Unveiled:
SECRETS TO A MARRIAGE THAT LASTS FOREVER

Stanley Padgett

Copyright © 2018 by Stanley Padgett

Unveiled: SECRETS TO A MARRIAGE THAT LASTS FOREVER

All rights reserved. No part of this publication may be reproduced, distributed, or transmitted in any form or by any means, including photocopying, recording, or other electronic or mechanical methods, without the prior written permission of the publisher, except in the case of brief quotations embodied in critical reviews and certain other noncommercial uses permitted by copyright law. For permission requests, write to the publisher, addressed "Attention: Permissions Coordinator," at info@beyondpublishing.net

Quantity sales special discounts are available on quantity purchases by corporations, associations, and others. For details, contact the publisher at the address above.

Orders by U.S. trade bookstores and wholesalers. Email info@BeyondPublishing.net

The Beyond Publishing Speakers Bureau can bring authors to your live event. For more information or to book an event contact the Beyond Publishing Speakers Bureau speak@BeyondPublishing.net

The Author can be reached directly BeyondPublishing.net/Author-Stan-Padgett

Manufactured and printed in the United States of America distributed globally by BeyondPublishing.net

New York | Los Angeles | London | Sydney

Softcover ISBN: 978-1-949873-19-1

ebook ISBN: 978-1-949873-18-4

Foreword

I've been blessed to be married to my high school sweetheart, Linda, for over 42 years. We got engaged less than three months after she turned 16 (I was only 17). We got married at 17 and 18. Our marriage survived the birth of our first child during college, the birth of our second child during law school, the birth of our third child while I was working crazy hours as a young lawyer, raising three children while starting my own law firm, and the deaths of two grandsons. Today, our favorite activity is anything we can do together. We enjoy each other that much.

The marriage deck was stacked against us. So, why did our marriage survive and thrive? If you think it's all been sunshine and roses; not quite. Our first apartment was $78 a month. We were struggling students raising small children for the first six years of our marriage. At 17 and 18, we were children ourselves. And at times, I was a jerk.

Fortunately for us, Linda grew up faster than I did, and she was patient until I caught up. During our marriage, we became very active in our church, and I had the opportunity to serve in positions that required me to spend many years working with adults and couples on marriage and relationship issues.

I read and studied and tried to sort out what made sense and what really worked. I discovered simple principles and practices common to powerful, satisfying relationships that can be taught and learned. Linda and I learned those lessons through the school of hard knocks.

This book is what we learned about how to build a Diamond Marriage; one that will stand the test of time; because marriages should be forever too.

Stan Padgett, December 2018

Acknowledgements

This book compiles life lessons taught to me by my family (my wife Linda, my children Marc, Maria and Brian, and my many grandchildren), my work as a trial lawyer, and my church service working with single, married and divorced adults. Over the years, I learned more than they know from my dear friends Robert Howell and Marvin Slovacek, who taught with purpose and by example. They lived the principles they taught every day. I also want to thank the many people I've had the opportunity to teach and work with on marriage issues. I always learned more than I taught. This book is dedicated to every couple who wants their marriage to last forever, and to every child everywhere because they all deserve to grow up in a loving home with both of their parents.

Contents

Chapter 1
Before You Say "I Do": The Questions You Should Ask Each Other ... 09

Chapter 2
Don't Let Your Wedding Cause Your Divorce ... 43

Chapter 3
Plan Your Marriage ... 51

Chapter 4
The Honeymoon is Over - Now What? ... 59

Chapter 5
Your First Baby Changes Everything ... 77

Chapter 6
Things That Can Break You ... 95

Chapter 7
Men and Women are Different ... 111

Chapter 8
A Diamond Marriage: Because Marriage Should Be Forever Too ... 121

Unveiled:
SECRETS TO A
MARRIAGE
THAT LASTS FOREVER

Chapter 1

Before You Say "I Do":
THE QUESTIONS YOU SHOULD ASK EACH OTHER

You're excited. You have a deep emotional relationship and want to be with that person forever. What do you really need to know about someone before you commit to spend the rest of your life with them? What questions should you ask each other before you say I do?

Many people believe being in love means everything will work out. The divorce rate in America suggests that's not true. According to the American Psychological Association, 40 to 50 percent of first marriages in the U.S. end in divorce. The statistics on second and subsequent marriages are even more dismal; 60 to 75 percent of those marriages end in divorce.

In more than a decade of working with couples on marital issues, a few things showed up with startling regularity. One of the partners would say, "That's not the person I married," or "I guess I didn't know them that well." They didn't realize they really were saying, "That's not the person I thought I married," or, "I guess I didn't pay attention to the clues or my feelings."

There's an old saying that men go into marriage thinking women will stay the same, women go into marriage thinking they can change (or save) the men, and they're both wrong. Let's explore both of those ideas briefly.

When a woman is dating and actively looking for a mate, she tends to take care of herself and be careful to present her best self. The man looks at her and thinks, "I could enjoy waking up to her every day." One of my former assistants had a favorite saying, "Men are shallow as spit." Even if it's true, knowledge is power ladies.

Men either follow that same approach or just start out being jerks. Nice guys often complain that girls like to date bad boys. If your guy is a lazy, selfish slob with no education, no ambition, and no job when you meet him, what makes you think he's going to change for you?

You may have been burned by dates or potential mates who were not at all as advertised. Internet dating magnifies those problems. Have you ever reviewed a profile, thought it was interesting, and the picture turned out to be 20 years old or of someone else, or none of the information on the profile was true?

Those types of experiences have left many singles frustrated, angry, jaded, and skeptical. In the mid-1990s, another former assistant said, "Men are like parking spots. The good ones are taken, and the rest are handicapped."

Other amazing single men and women are looking for the right person too, but they're as cautious and skeptical as you. You need patience to find the right person to marry. Patience means time to see them in different situations: in private, in public, in a restaurant, with his or her friends, with his or her family, with your friends, with your family, and in stressful situations.

Stress doesn't shape character; it reveals character. Someone who is kind and considerate in stressful situations almost certainly will be that way every day. But even finding a person of good character doesn't mean they're the right person for you to marry. Many couples divorce because they get infatuated before they get educated (about each other).

Each person comes into a relationship with a value system based on their upbringing, beliefs and prior experiences. Those values and beliefs are critical to their ability to create a lasting, loving marriage.

Many people aren't consciously aware of their own values, or how strongly they hold certain values. Discovering your own values and how strongly you hold each one is key to finding a marriage partner you can enjoy being with forever. Try this exercise.

Step 1

In the space below, list every characteristic of your ideal mate; someone who fills your deepest needs. If a woman is absolutely committed to having children, some of those characteristics will be things like wants or loves children, patient, and great father or great role model.

Imagine you're on Amazon, and the person you order will be delivered to you in three days. Describe them in so much detail that when you open the package and they step out, you'll be delighted, but not surprised.

_____

_____

_____

_____

_____

_____

_____

_____

_____

_____

_____

_____

Step 2

Everything you listed above is what your ideal mate "should" be. Go back to the list and circle the two or three (no more than five) qualities they "must" be for you to be happy and fulfilled. The list you made will be unique to you, and so will the "must-be" items on your list.

Step 3

How many people do you know who go through the same failed relationship over and over? The name of the person keeps changing, but each one is very much alike; they share the same characteristics. That happens because they've never been taught to identify what they need and what they can't tolerate.

This may help illustrate the principle. No matter what car you drive, before you got that car, how many of that make and model did you see on the road? As soon as you got the car, how many of them did you see? You saw more of them once you owned one, because your subconscious mind looked for them to validate your purchase.

In the space below, list every characteristic of the mate from hell; the person you absolutely cannot live with. I once did this exercise with a group of singles over age 30, most of whom were divorced. When I asked them to do this, a lady raised her hand and said, "Can I just write my ex-husband's name?" No, you can't.

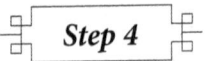
Step 4

Everything you listed above describes what your mate "should not be." Go back to the list and circle the two to three (no more than five) qualities they "must not be" for you to be happy and fulfilled. These are the deal breakers. No matter how many other good qualities they have, you just can't live with these. This list will also be unique to you, and so will the "must not be" items on your list.

If you're just starting your journey to find your ideal mate, take the second list and put it away. You don't need it anymore. You just needed to identify clearly what you can't live with long-term. Then, take your first list, and read it out loud in front of your mirror every day for 30 days, with as much emotion as you can, and with a feeling of certainty you'll receive the person you listed. Then, put that list in your pocket or purse, and read it out loud at least once a week. Just like in the car example, your subconscious mind will begin to look for someone with those characteristics.

Step 5

You need to make one more list: who you need to become to attract the person on your first list. Then, go to work on yourself. Benjamin Franklin identified 13 virtues he wanted to develop or improve. He wrote each one on a card. Each week put one of those cards in his pocket and worked on that virtue all week. At the end of the week, he put that card on the bottom of the stack and put the card for the next virtue in his pocket. With 13 virtues, he went through his list of virtues four times a year (13 x 4 = 52 weeks). Do you think being intentional about improving in a single area for four weeks over the course of a year would result in significant improvement? Now, imagine doing that year after year, and picture the results.

Many people struggle with weight. If your ideal mate "must be" physically active and love the outdoors, how likely are you to attract that person if you're 100 pounds overweight and rarely exercise? What if you were intentional about making lifestyle changes for the specific purpose of attracting the person you would be deliriously happy to spend your life with? What if your ideal mate "must be" well-read, and you haven't read a book or a newspaper in years? Can you become what you need to be to attract that person? Of course.

Am I suggesting you change who you are? Not at all. If you're not willing to change characteristics that make it unlikely for you to find a mate who meets your "must be" list, your list isn't real, and you haven't dug deeply enough into your own beliefs and needs. Stop playing on the surface and get brutally honest with yourself. Until you're honest with yourself, you're not capable of being truly honest with another person in a way that supports the love necessary for a marriage to last forever.

When you're trying to decide if the person you're attracted to or in a relationship with is someone you can be married to forever, you need to have them go through the exercise you just did (without giving them any more instructions than you had before you did each exercise).

The "musts" and "must nots" you each identified are your core values. If any of your core values are in direct conflict, nothing else matters. You can't have a lasting, loving, fulfilling marriage with that person. Let me explain with an example.

If a woman's core value is that she must have children, and her man's core value is he must never bring children into this world, there is no way for both of them to have one of their core needs met. They're fundamentally incompatible. That sounds harsh, but how did it feel when you read it?

That's a long introduction to the primary subject of this chapter, what do you need to know before you say "I do."

The four conversations every couple needs to have before they say I do are sex, money, children, and religion. Those conversations are even more important in second or subsequent marriages, because both partners come with established patterns related to sex and money, and children of either spouse present huge potential problems in creating a new, stable, happy family.

Let's start with the first marriage for both partners. For those couples, the discussion reveals their level of emotional maturity and how ready they are to be part of a new family unit. In *The 7 Habits of Highly Effective People*, Stephen R. Covey describes three levels on the "Maturity Continuum" from lowest to highest: dependence, independence, and interdependence.

If you haven't read the book, you should. In fact, both of you should. Covey teaches that as a child, we're totally dependent on others emotionally and for our very survival. For a variety of reasons, some people never grow out of that state.

An emotionally dependent person is unlikely to form a lasting, loving marriage. They simply don't have the emotional maturity to make the decisions and consistently take the actions that produce a forever marriage.

Most people grow from being dependent to being independent, physically, mentally, emotionally, and financially. They can take care of their own needs. In today's society, college seems to last longer, and young men and women seem to stay at home with their parents longer (or move out and move back home). If you believe financial independence mirrors emotional independence, be very cautious about a potential mate who is 25 years old and still living at home.

With all its challenges, America is still the land of opportunity; the field of dreams. Many people are too busy wasting time and complaining about what other people have and how they got it to do the work themselves. Success leaves clues, and success requires sacrifice. An enormous body of success literature exists that can feed the mind of any ambitious person. A suggested reading list appears at the end of this book.

I believe in education. I received a Bachelor of Science in government from Auburn University at Montgomery (1979) and a law degree from Duke University School of Law (1982). Even with those degrees, I'm convinced anyone who reads all of the books on the reading list and applies the principles in them will have received a finer education than any college or university in America can provide—at a tiny fraction of the time and cost. The knowledge will be practical and immediately usable.

How many college graduates do you know who can only find minimum wage or low-paying jobs and still have tens or hundreds of thousands of dollars of student loan debt hanging over their heads? Even if you're going to college, what if you took some of the time you're partying, playing, or spending on social media and invested in yourself? Read the books on the list. Test whether what you can learn for a few hundred dollars can make you wealthy beyond anything your college professors can even imagine.

Two independent people can create a forever marriage. That doesn't mean you don't need each other. From a place of emotional independence, you can decide to rely on someone else some of the time, and have the strength to share with them when they need it.

Covey's highest state of emotional maturity is interdependence. It's the difference between dependence (you take care of me) to independence (I can take care of me) to interdependence (we take care of each other). Isn't that the definition of a successful marriage? *I don't have to be with you. I choose to be with you because I love, trust, and respect you, and being with you brings me joy.* You're better together than either of you would be alone.

When you find that person, marry them and hang on tight. When I met Linda, I instantly knew I wanted to be with her. (I'm still not sure what she saw in me, but I'm eternally grateful). Over the years, we've grown through all of the stages and now both know we're better together than either of us would be alone, and our grandchildren can't imagine us any other way.

Back to our four topics - sex, money, children, and religion.

Let's start with sex. In first marriages, it's still possible that one or both partners come into the marriage with little or no sexual experience and no children. For reasons of religion, culture, or personal standards, one or both of the couple may not have been sexually active—even with their potential mate. Even if you don't have any experience, you still need to talk about sex. It may be a difficult or awkward conversation but have it anyway.

If neither of you are experienced (or one of you isn't), there are lots of non-pornographic resources to teach you what you don't know. One young couple I know got a copy of "Sex for Dummies" and massage oil as a wedding present. Please don't think what you've heard from friends, read in **50 Shades of Grey,** or saw in a porno flick are what everyone does. Sex in marriage is the ultimate expression of love, trust, intimacy, and vulnerability. It's special and sacred. Treat it that way.

In all of these discussions, be brutally honest with yourself and gently honest with your partner. Be open about your fears, your needs, what you want, and what you're comfortable doing. You might consider starting with your understanding and expectations. What do you think or understand your physical and emotional needs to be?

You might talk about how a man's motor goes from zero to 60 in three seconds flat and hers doesn't. He's a sprinter, and she runs marathons. Men need to slow down and take the time to be sure you both finish the race. If neither of you are experienced, you may not know much about your needs and preferences. Some of that will have to wait until after the wedding night.

If you don't fit into the above discussion, you've probably already experienced each other's needs and preferences. If either of you needs more or is uncomfortable with anything you've already done, talk about it before you say "I do." If you're not honest about it now, someone is going to be very disappointed after the wedding.

I've worked with many married couples for whom addiction to pornography created huge problems. Initially, it was largely a male problem, with men acting out or expecting things from their wives they'd seen porn stars do.

Unfortunately, pornography has become so prevalent and readily available virtually everyone with a smartphone has some level of exposure, and women are becoming addicted too. Pornography has become so pervasive in our society it may be unrealistic to expect to find any 18-year-old in America who hasn't been exposed.

According to the American Addiction Centers, Inc. ("AAC"), "Viewing pornography can have negative consequences on teenagers down the line, affecting both their psychological and physical wellbeing. These ramifications include:

- Increase in high-risk behaviors.
- Skewed view of the world.
- Decrease in ability to build healthy relationships.
- Normalization of sexual violence.
- Increase in aggression towards women.
- Research reveals that teenagers exposed to sexually explicit websites are more likely to be promiscuous and more likely to have used alcohol or other intoxicating substances during their last sexual encounter. This puts them at a higher risk for developing a substance abuse disorder or mental health disorder. See *www.pyschguidelines.com*.

In addition to the sexual problems created by pornography, the statistics on the number of children under 18 who've been sexually assaulted at some point are appalling. The National Sexual Violence Research

Center says, "One in four girls and one in six boys will be sexually abused before they turn 18 years old." See *www.nsvrc.org/statistics*. My experience suggests sexual abuse may be even more widespread than those statistics suggest.

The overwhelming majority of child sexual assaults are by people known by the child; someone the parent or caregiver trusted enough to leave alone with the child. The Rape, Abuse & Incest National Network, the nation's largest anti-sexual violence organization, indicates that 93 percent of child victims of sexual abuse know their attacker. See *www.rainn.org/statistics/children-and-teens*.

Child victims of sexual abuse often are sworn to secrecy, threatened, or told their attacker will harm them or other members of their family if they tell. They may develop beliefs sex is dirty, they can't make any noise during sex because someone might hear, or they can't talk about it. Worse still, when they try to tell a parent or teacher and aren't believed, they lose the ability to trust, because none of the people who should have protected them knew or cared enough to do so.

When children lose the ability to trust, it's hard to recover, and since trust is one of the pillars of love, it makes deep, loving relationships difficult (but not impossible) to develop. Most children, by nature, are physically affectionate. They bond with their parents by being held close, where they feel safe and secure. Sexual assault destroys that feeling of trust and with it, the ability and desire to physically connect with another person.

Most men probably have no idea how many women have been sexually assaulted. Neither did I until after years of working with women who were victims of sexual assault. A few months ago, I explained to a female friend my surprise at the number of women who were victims of sexual assault. She asked what percentage of women I thought had been sexually assaulted, and I told her 30 to 50 percent.

She said I wasn't even close, and if she was with a hundred women and one of them said she had been sexually assaulted, every woman in the room would believe her, because it had happened to them, too. She then told me about three times she'd been sexually assaulted before she was 18 with one coming within a few seconds of rape. We've been close for many years, and I never knew. She suffered in silence for 50 years.

Sexual assault often affects the victim's ability to form healthy relationships and healthy sexual practices, even with their mate. I've worked with many women in their 30s, 40s, and even 50s who still struggled with issues related to childhood sexual assaults.

The statistics on sexual assault are so overwhelming it may be best if both partners (but especially men) assume their spouse or prospective spouse has been sexually assaulted at some point and be loving and patient enough to give each other time to heal and develop trust.

Depending on the nature of the sexual assault/s/ and how long they continued, one or both of you may need professional counseling before marriage. If you're struggling with sexual intimacy before marriage, work it out. Your sexual assault may affect your interest in sex with your partner **and** your ability to be emotionally available to your children.

One friend who talked with me about this book described how his first wife's sister has been sexually assaulted by her step-father for years and had been destroyed by the experience. His ex-wife brought her anger against her stepfather into their marriage. It destroyed their marriage and affected their sons.

She transferred her anger at her stepfather onto her sons and never bonded with them. They grew up not understanding why their mother didn't love them. Can you imagine the challenges a woman will face in a relationship with a man who grew up in that toxic environment?

Ladies, you don't understand your own power. For you to have the love, joy, passion, and connection you want in your marriage, your husband must be willing to be vulnerable to you. He's usually not physically vulnerable to you, but he's incredibly vulnerable to what you say.

A man's ego is like a balloon blown up large enough to thin the skin. A prick with a sharp word pops the balloon. When it explodes, you lose much of his willingness to be vulnerable to you, because he can't trust you with the vulnerable parts of himself.

Here's an example from our lives. Linda and I were married after my freshman year of college. We had our first child during my junior year of college. Part of the process of applying to law school is taking the Law School Admissions Test (LSAT). A friend of mine at Auburn University at Montgomery took the LSAT the year before I did. At that time, the highest possible score on the LSAT was 800. Her score of 705 ranked in the 95th percentile nationwide and was celebrated in our department at school.

The following year, I took the LSAT. I opened the letter at home with my young bride to find a score of 755; in the 99th percentile nationwide. I was ecstatic, until she said something like, "That doesn't seem like a big deal." My balloon burst, and I never cared about the score again. It was good enough to get me into Duke Law School, but it didn't matter to her, so it didn't matter to me.

I never told her how her words made me feel, and when she reads this book, she probably won't remember it at all. I do, and it happened 40 years ago. Why did it matter so much? Because she was the only person whose opinion mattered to me.

When someone is completely vulnerable to you (emotionally naked), handle their heart with care, and it will be yours forever. Divorce statistics suggest too few couples treat each other's hearts with the tender care they deserve. When you get hurt, you build up scar tissue. Scar tissue is less sensitive, less giving, and less forgiving.

Linda and I were married with children at the time, but were still children ourselves. We now have a granddaughter who is older than Linda was when I proposed to her. I can't think of anything else like that she's said in our 42 years of marriage. She probably has dozens of things like that I've said to her, but is too kind and loving to ever tell me about them. She's the best thing that ever happened to me, and I love her more every day.

Let's talk about how we create deep, powerful memories. My dad was born at home on a small farm in rural South Carolina in 1930, during the Great Depression. He left home at 18 and joined the Air Force. During the Korean War, he was stationed in the Philippines. He went home to South Carolina after the Air Force and went to college on the GI Bill. He graduated from the University of South Carolina (the real USC), with a degree in civil engineering; the first person in his family to graduate from college.

My mother was born in Columbia, South Carolina in 1931; the fourteenth child in her family. Her mother and father both died when she was six. None of her older siblings could take her, so she grew up in a Methodist orphanage. If you imagine life in an orphanage during the Great Depression as austere and miserable, you're right.

She spent the rest of her childhood in the orphanage, until she graduated from high school and went to work as an operator for Southern Bell. If you ever watched *The Andy Griffith Show* or old movies, you may have seen the old phone board with operators pulling cables out and plugging them in to connect calls. That was my mom.

My parents married in 1956. Dad went to work as a civil engineer for what was then the federal Bureau of Public Roads (now the Department of Transportation). I was born in 1957, and we moved about every six months for his job. We lived in South Carolina, North Carolina, the State of Washington, and Virginia. We moved to Frankfort, Kentucky when I was about four. I started first grade in Frankfort in 1963 in an old brick school building.

On November 22, 1963, the intercom clicked on during lunch, and the principal said, "The President of the United States has been shot." The intercom clicked off. It clicked on again just before school was out. The principal said, "The President of the United States is dead." President John F. Kennedy died in Dallas that day. I remember very little else about first grade, but those words were burned into my memory and have remained fresh for over 50 years.

Some of you have vivid memories of January 28, 1986, the day the space shuttle Challenger exploded with a school teacher, Christa McAuliffe, aboard. Even more of you remember September 11, 2001, the day terrorists attacked our nation and killed more than 3,000 Americans. You probably remember details about where you were, who you were with and what you were doing when you learned about those events, because the powerful emotions they evoked created permanent links in your memory.

Thoughtless words spoken by the one we love most at a critical time create those same powerful emotional links. The words are rarely forgotten and may have an impact never intended or understood by the speaker. If you want to be emotionally connected to your spouse in a deep and intimate way, make sure to engage your mind before you open your mouth.

The old saying, "sticks and stones may break my bones, but words can never hurt me" is just plain wrong. Your words do damage you can't see. Once you hurt your spouse deeply—even unintentionally—they emotionally withdraw to protect themselves. You may become frustrated by the lack of connection and never recognize you caused it by violating their trust and hurting them when they were vulnerable to you.

We moved to Bowling Green, Kentucky when I was in third grade and stayed there until after my junior year of high school. While we were there, my Dad started his own engineering company with a partner. After my junior year, he and his partner decided to open a branch office in Montgomery, Alabama. We moved to Alabama in the summer of 1974. My parents actually left before I did. They moved while I went on a two-week high school Spanish Club trip to Mexico. I drove to Alabama after the trip.

I had worked at Burger King in Bowling Green, and a few months after we moved to Montgomery, I got a job at the local Burger King. That's where I met Linda. We didn't live very far apart, but she attended a rival high school because we lived on opposite sides of the school boundary. The first time I saw her, I was working, and she came in on a date with one of the other guys who worked there.

In those days, Burger King employees wore orange and yellow polyester shirts and orange and yellow paper hats. As soon as they walked away from the counter, I turned to the guy next to me who had called her by name, grabbed two handfuls of his yellow and orange polyester shirt and said, "Who is that?"

I know exactly what she was wearing that day. That was her last date with the other guy, and her last date with anyone else ever. By the way, a fellow has got to have game to attract a beautiful girl while wearing an orange and yellow polyester shirt and a paper hat (just sayin').

Let's talk about money. Many young couples get married expecting to live the same lifestyle their parents created after 30 years of work. Men used to be taught they were responsible to provide for their wife and children. In many cultures and households, that's still true. As a result, they often base their identity and sense of self-worth on their ability to provide for their family. Can you imagine the effect on a man's self-esteem if his wife attacks his ability to provide for her and their children when he's doing all he can?

There are as many ways to handle money in a relationship as there are relationships, so the odds you have identical experiences with money are slim to none. Your cultural or religious backgrounds may influence your attitudes and feelings about money. Is money good or bad? Is having money good or bad? Is being frugal a virtue or vice? Does money grow on trees, or doesn't it? Financial issues show up on most lists of causes of divorce, so shouldn't you work through them before you get married?

Dave Ramsey is a popular author and speaker on financial issues and created "Financial Peace University." If Linda and I had seen that as newlyweds, I would have retired ten years ago, and it would have been the only present each of my children would have gotten when they graduated from high school.

Dave Ramsey's savers and spenders approach is an amazing and funny way to learn financial principles and budgeting. Savers and spenders have fundamentally different approaches to handling money. Two savers in a marriage works really well. If you get two spenders, that's a financial disaster looking for a place to happen. If you get one saver and one spender, sit back and watch the sparks fly.

Because financial challenges are one of the primary causes of divorce, it's important to do everything possible to take that stress out of your relationship. You simply must be aligned on financial issues. What are your financial expectations? How are you going to handle money? Are you going to have one account, two separate accounts, or two separate accounts and one joint account you both fund? Who's going to handle the account? Who's going to balance it? Are you going to budget? Do you know how to budget? What kind of budget are you going to use? Are you going to use a Dave Ramsey cash-based budget? Are you going to save? If so, how and how much? Are you going to give back?

Take a moment to write your answers to those questions in the space below. Then, have your prospective spouse answer them. Compare and discuss your answers.

_____
_____
_____
_____
_____
_____
_____
_____
_____
_____
_____
_____
_____
_____
_____

Whether you come from a religious background or not, the principle of tithing works. Whether you tithe to a church or a charity, giving with a glad heart allows God or the Universe to bless you with more. When you give just because you expect something in return, you might as well not give. A gift given with an attitude of gratitude and a feeling of abundance attracts good things. The Law of Attraction is real. If you haven't read The Secret, by Rhonda Byrne, you should. It's on the reading list.

One young couple asked me how they should build a budget. I suggested the following:

Step 1: Pay 10 percent of your gross income to your church or a charity.

Step 2: Pay 10 percent of your gross income into a permanent savings account for you.

Step 3: Pay five percent of your gross income into a memory fund - money you spend every year making special memories as a family.

Step 4: Pay your bills and live on the rest.

I recommend couples take Dave Ramsey's "Financial Peace University" course and classes together. As of December 2018, the video course is $129.99 and can only be bought with a debit card. Dave doesn't believe in debt, so he won't take credit cards. I can't stress enough how valuable this course will be to you—even if you decide not to get married or are already married. You have a choice. Either you learn to control money, or it will control you.

Here's something to think about. How many people do you know who lost a job or got sick and didn't get a paycheck for a week or longer? How many of them (or you) were financially desperate even before they missed that paycheck? Would you feel different if you lost a job and had $10,000 or six months of all your living expenses in savings? You would, and so would your spouse.

Money in savings reduces or eliminates the stress of having no way to pay your rent, your car payment, or buy groceries. You also don't suffer a loss of self-esteem that affects your confidence as you search for a new job, or the feelings of inadequacy you both may feel if you can't provide for yourselves or your family.

If a man's identity is tied up in being able to provide, he may feel insecure at a time when his wife most needs his emotional strength to feel secure. When he can't give her his emotional strength and she feels insecure, she may react to the insecurity verbally or by withdrawing physically or emotionally. Those little steps lead to big fractures.

If you've followed the four-step pattern above, you've created a permanent savings fund you can fall back on in rough times. You still take the five percent memory fund and spend it every year. At the end of your life, what's important will be the memories you made with the people you love. Whether you take a family vacation or go on a mission trip isn't important. What you do together as a family strengthens the bonds between you. Those bonds strengthen your forever marriage.

Many people get caught up in material possessions. A number of years ago, a good friend of mine and her husband were called to serve a three-year church mission outside the United States. He had done very well in real estate, and they had accumulated lots of nice stuff. They could only take about two thousand pounds of goods with them.

They put her baby grand piano in storage and sold virtually everything else. She said she had a very hard time getting rid of the things they'd accumulated over a lifetime, until she realized she had never seen a hearse followed by a U-Haul truck. That mental image put material possessions in context for her (and for me).

As newlyweds, we moved into a $78 per month apartment the landlord had been using to store old appliances, and we had to renovate it ourselves. The landlord cleaned out the appliances and gave us a month's free rent and the paint and materials so we could fix it up before we got married. My parents lived in a nice apartment complex that replaced the carpets for new tenants. They gave us the carpet out of an apartment, and we cut it to fit our new place. We put that used wall-to-wall carpet in our first apartment and were delighted with it. We never expected to live like our parents (but then, they didn't live very fancy, either).

Neither of our families had much money, and neither of us got any training in how to budget or save or handle money. Like most young adults (and we're really stretching the definition of adults to apply it to us at 18 and 17), our only money model was our parents. High schools then (and now, so far as I understand) didn't teach practical money skills, which is a terrible disservice to our children. How many of you have recently had to deal with money issues? How many of you have recently used anything you learned in biology or geometry? You get the point.

Linda and I never lived extravagantly, and she certainly never demanded expensive things. I was fortunate to get a "Walmart" kind of girl, instead of a "Neiman Marcus" (needless markup) kind of girl. Better yet, she doesn't like jewelry (woo-hoo!). Still, without a budget, there always seemed to be more month than money, even after I started practicing law and making what we thought was good money.

We made one very distinct change from the way my parents handled money. My mother was a stay-at-home mom until after I left home, so my dad earned all the money. She always had to ask my dad for money—even for groceries—and it felt wrong to me. I promised myself my wife would never have to ask me for money, and she never has. I've never carried or kept our checkbook. Linda handled our banking and kept and balanced the checkbook and does now with all our businesses and my law practice.

For most of the time since our third child was born, she's been a stay-at-home wife, mother, and grandmother— she's the best Nana in the world, just ask our grandchildren. At times, she felt like she wasn't contributing to our household financially and would say, "It's your money." So far as I can remember, I never said that in 42 years of marriage, never felt that way, and gently corrected her any time she said it. I remember how that made my mom feel, and I never wanted Linda to have that feeling. She is the greatest gift in my life, and I work every day to remind her what she means to me. I hope she knows by now.

The third key topic is children. Where to begin? There are lots of important questions about children. Do we want them? How many? When? How far apart? How are we going to raise them? How are we going to educate them? Do we raise them in any religion? Which one? How strictly are we going to follow the teachings of that faith? What standards of behavior do we expect in our home? How do we enforce those standards?

What are the consequences for bad behavior? How is discipline going to be done? Who's going to do it? How do we pay for the children? Do we give them an allowance? Do we pay for their first car, first house, or college education? Do we require them to work? At what age? What are they expected to do around the house? What extracurricular activities will they be allowed to participate in? How many extracurricular activities will each child be allowed to participate in? You get the idea.

In the space below, write your ideal answers to each of those questions, and ask your prospective spouse to do the same. Then compare and discuss your answers.

_____
_____
_____
_____
_____
_____
_____
_____
_____
_____
_____
_____
_____
_____
_____

Some of these questions will be deal breakers for one or both of you; core values on your "must be" or "must have" lists. If one of your "must be" or "must have" items directly conflicts with a "must not be" or "cannot have" for your prospective spouse, your relationship is already in trouble.

Today's society provides so many options in terms of education, career, business ownership, travel, and freedom one or both of you may not want children. You don't want the responsibilities, restrictions, financial burdens, or loss of freedom children bring. If the other one must have children, please stop now. Don't plan a wedding or a life together until you understand if these are core values or just something you don't want right now.

Some religions don't believe in birth control or in limiting the number of children in a family. We'll get to the religion discussion a little later on, so put that aside right now. If both of you want children, but one of you wants to delay having children for a period of time or until a specific event occurs (for example, two years or after graduation from college), you should be able to work that out.

The partner who wants to delay having children may have grown up in poor or modest circumstances and emotionally linked having children (or having children early in a marriage) to financial problems or marital problems. If having children is a core value for either of you, commitments made about the delay must be absolute.

If the partner asking for the delay moves the date or event or later decides they really don't want children at all, they have fundamentally breached their partner's trust in a way that probably ends the marriage. They promised to meet their partner's core value of having children and reneged.

Questions about children have even more significance in a second or subsequent marriage (or if either spouse brings a child to a first marriage). At least one ecclesiastical leader I respect immensely has seen so many problems with second marriages involving children he counsels parents not to marry or live together until their last child leaves home. He hasn't been very successful getting couples to follow that counsel but based on the outcomes he's seen of couples he counseled before marriage, many of them probably regret not listening.

Why is it so much harder to make a marriage last when either spouse brings children to the marriage? One reason may be that the number of people who have to get along is multiplied, often by large numbers. For example, if both of you have been married before and each have two children, you now have six people in the house with different needs, experiences, standards, and styles of communication. In addition, unless your ex-spouses are deceased or in jail, you have to deal with two other adults (or so-called adults—typically referred to as the crazy exes).

Children add to the complexity of marriage because they're born master manipulators of adult behavior. If you doubt that statement, consider a newborn baby. So far as we know, their wants are simple: food, warmth, lack of pain or discomfort and security. If you already have experience caring for a newborn, there were times when the baby was fed, burped, dry, and not sick or otherwise in any discomfort. You wrap them in a blanket, rock them to sleep, and they lay still and content in your arms.

As soon as you lay them down in a crib or bassinet, they immediately wake up and begin to cry. You pick them up, rock them back to sleep, and lay them down, only to have them wake up again and cry. They repeat the pattern until you give up and hold them while they sleep. What just happened?

The newborn felt the lack of human contact (or warmth or connection) and responded by crying. You responded by picking the infant up and giving them what they needed. Their behavior may have been purely instinctive, but it worked! They unconsciously manipulated adult behavior!

Some parents never recognize the pattern and allow it to continue until their children become toddlers and consciously manipulate adults by crying, screaming, or throwing tantrums to get what they want. Parents who fail to correct that behavior early end up raising what members of my generation call spoiled brats, instead of respectful children. Spoiled brats and teenagers share at least one common characteristic; they're even better manipulators of adult behavior than newborns; and even more difficult to deal with in second or subsequent marriages.

You may have time-sharing arrangements, limitations on your ability to move out of the county, state, or country, different parenting styles, different standards of behavior, different consequences, and so forth. Go back through the list of questions about children and think about them again in the context of a second marriage.

In the space below, write how bringing children into a marriage affects each of those questions, and ask your prospective spouse to do the same. Then, compare and discuss your lists.

_____
_____
_____
_____
_____
_____
_____
_____
_____
_____

Consider your own experience if you grew up in a single-parent or step-parent household, (or if you grew up in a home with both of your biological or adoptive parents, ask your friends who grew up in single-parent or step-parent homes), how they felt and how they were treated. Linda's mom and dad were divorced when she was young, and she didn't see her dad for several years. When she was about ten, she and her younger sister went back to live with her dad, his new wife, her two daughters, and their son together.

Linda is very intuitive and knew none of them except her dad wanted them to be a part of their family. The children said so straight out. The step-mom said all the right things, but Linda knew on every issue, every time, her stepmom would always choose her children. To keep the peace, her dad sided with his new wife.

Linda went back to live with her mom when she was about 15 and was never again close with her dad. On his deathbed nearly 40 years later, he apologized to Linda and her sister and said he wished he'd done things differently when they were young. His apology came way too late to salvage their relationship.

I'm not saying that second marriages can't work, only that they're even more work than first marriages if they're going to last forever. Answering the questions about blending families is hard, and living the answers and agreements even harder. It can be done, but requires both parents to be committed, consistent, considerate, and patient.

Let's talk about a few specifics. How do you deal with the issues caused by child-sharing arrangements with ex-spouses? Children want things and don't want restrictions or limitations (even though they desperately need them). How do you handle an ex-spouse giving the children material possessions you don't approve of or can't afford to give them, or allowing them to do things that don't meet the standards in your home? What is your new spouse's role going to be in disciplining your children? If your answer is, "I don't know," you're being honest. There are no easy answers.

To have a marriage that lasts forever, you must become one family with one set of standards, and both parents must be able to enforce those standards with all of the children. You discipline your kids your way, and I'll discipline mine my way, is a recipe for disaster. By refusing to allow your spouse to give direction and impose agreed-upon consequences on your children, you're teaching your children they don't need to respect your spouse. Any man or woman worth having will refuse to live that way. In addition, the children will be bitter and miserable and will make your life bitter and miserable.

People get divorced for many reasons, at least one of which is that they can't get along. Do you think it's likely that's going to get better when they divorce? In a perfect world, parents would act like adults after divorce and do what's best for the children. If you believe that's what really happens, talk to any divorce lawyer or family court judge, and you'll learn it just ain't so.

In divorce, children often become weapons or poker chips. One spouse deliberately tries to poison the children's relationship with their other parent or the other parent's new significant other or spouse. At times, the fight over time sharing is really over the amount of child support one ex-spouse has to pay the other. The stories are horrific, and the children always end up the losers.

Children deserve better. They deserve parents who have a Diamond Marriage; one that is strong, stable, loving, and safe. That's why I wrote this book.

I've actually seen a few couples get along better after divorce than they ever did while they were married. Unfortunately, in every one of those situations, the truce ended as soon as one of them found someone new. Whether through jealousy or insecurity, the now-jilted ex-spouse fell back into the normal pattern, and the children lost again.

Discussing children before you say "I do" gets both of you on the same page on an issue fundamental to the success and happiness of your marriage in the short term and the long term.

The last topic you need to discuss is religion, especially if religion or religious practice is a core value for either of you. A marriage involving different faiths or very different levels of commitment to faith presents special challenges. The greater the difference in the beliefs of each faith and the greater the difference in the level of commitment to faith, the greater the challenges.

The starting point in preparing to say "I do" is a direct conversation about your respective faiths. Be open, and spend time studying the faith of your prospective spouse; not for the purpose of being converted to their faith, but to understand your spouse on a deep level. Based on the number of adherents, the four largest religions in the world are: Christianity, Islam, Hinduism, and Buddhism. A surface-level comparison of those major religions reveals vast differences in teachings and practices.

In the United States, the three largest religions are Christianity, Judaism, and Islam. Included within the broad category of Christianity are Catholics and Protestants of innumerable varieties. Even though all of those religions base their theology on a belief in Jesus Christ, the varieties of their doctrines, practices, and expectations are nearly endless.

You don't need to become an expert in your prospective spouse's religion, you just need to understand its basic tenants, and evaluate how they align or conflict with your beliefs. Once you know where both of you stand on religion, you'll be able to answer many of the questions about the standards in your home and how your children will be raised. Find out if there are any deal breakers in this area before you say "I do" or have children.

You also should consider the impact of the religious beliefs and practices of your prospective in-laws, and how they will impact your relationship with them (and with your spouse). If the two of you have agreed not to follow the deeply held religious convictions of your or your spouse's parents, are both of you strong enough and committed enough to each other to withstand family pressure over time; especially when children come along?

Now that you've answered these questions and discussed them honestly with your partner, if you still want to get married, it's time to plan the wedding.

Chapter 2

DON'T LET YOUR WEDDING CAUSE YOUR DIVORCE

You said yes. You agreed to get married, you're excited, ecstatic, and elated. Now what? You immediately post the proposal and pictures of your ring on social media and begin basking in the glow of your friends and family. Not so fast. This is one of those times where thinking before acting can pay huge dividends.

What in the world am I talking about? What could be more important than letting everyone know the good news? A lot! Couples who fall in love and decide to get married come from an infinite number of cultures, religions, backgrounds, and family situations, many of which can make planning a wedding a nightmare.

Before you let everyone else in on the big news, take a breath, take a moment, and talk about what the two of you feel is the ideal wedding for you. This is the first major project you'll undertake as a couple, and it begins to set the pattern for your lives together. Will you counsel together and plan what's best for each of you individually and as a couple, or will you let family, friends, and other people interfere in your life together? The choices you make now reveal a lot about each of you and your emotional readiness to start a forever marriage.

You might say, "But my family has always wanted," or, "But my mother has always wanted," or "My dream has always been to have a fairytale wedding." When are you going to ask what you want or what your future spouse wants?

Ladies, please be aware that virtually no man wants a big, fancy wedding. He wants a wife, and that alone makes him exceptional. More and more men are reluctant to get married, and why not? They can get virtually all of the benefits of marriage without making the commitment.

You've found a man who's willing to buck the trend. Don't discourage him or make him feel he made the wrong decision. And despite popular culture, the wedding is not all about you. It's about both of you and the life you plan to have together *after* the wedding.

> The wedding culture in America sets marriages up to fail.

How many brides do you know who have been in tears on the way to the wedding chapel because the preparation has been so stressful they're absolutely miserable? The wedding culture in America consists of a complicated set of rituals that have overgrown what should be a simple and sacred joining of two people who love each other in a marriage that lasts forever.

Let's compare the required practices to the wedding culture practices. All U.S. states require a marriage license, the payment of a license fee, and an authorized person to perform the ceremony. Some require a three-day waiting period before the marriage can be performed. A few require a blood test or medical certificate. Most require one or more other people to sign the marriage license as witnesses to the ceremony. Authorized persons typically include judges, justices of the peace, clerks of court, notaries public, or members of the clergy. You can find a state by state chart of the requirements at *www.1800bride2b.com/articles/ marriagelaws_chart.htm.*

The sacred ceremony typically involves a set of wedding vows and takes about ten minutes to perform, even if the couple writes their own vows. The officiant knows what to do, so requires no special preparation for your wedding. Even writing your own vows takes a few hours at most. There are no dress standards or requirements for anyone to be present other than the officiant, the couple being married, and the number of witnesses needed to sign the marriage license.

If the couple dresses in their Sunday best, pays for the marriage license, and gets a small bouquet of flowers for the bride to hold, a wedding can cost under $100. They can easily stay focused on the reasons they decided to get married and the sacred vows they make to each other. (By the way, an engagement ring or wedding ring is a tradition, not a legal requirement).

Let's compare that simple sacred joining to the complex money machine the wedding industry in America has created. Here are some of the things the wedding culture says "must be" part of any real wedding. The list includes an engagement ring, engagement pictures, save-the-date announcements, wedding invitations, a gift registry, a bridal shower, a wedding dress, a florist, a rehearsal, a rehearsal dinner, a best man, groomsmen, a maid of honor, bridesmaids, a ring bearer, a flower girl, matching clothing for the groomsmen, bridesmaids dresses, floral arrangements, a rehearsal dinner venue, a wedding venue, a reception venue, decorations for the rehearsal dinner, wedding and reception venues, live music or a DJ for the rehearsal dinner and reception, music for the wedding ceremony, a wedding photographer to annoy people endlessly about hundreds of pictures almost no one will ever look at again, a videographer, a bachelor party, a bachelorette party, and probably many more I'm simply ignorant about.

Everything on the list (and all of the others I don't know about) have two things in common. They add absolutely nothing to the sacred vows the couple makes and have no bearing on whether the marriage lasts a month, a year, or forever. If the perfect wedding improved the odds of a marriage lasting forever, 40 to 50 percent of all first marriages in America wouldn't end in divorce.

What does the wedding culture do? It consumes all the time, energy, and money the couple and their families can afford—and often much more. It introduces enormous external stresses, expectations, and material nonsense into an essentially spiritual experience; the joining of two human beings in bonds of love and commitment. It dilutes and diminishes the couple's focus on each other and the sacred vows they're making.

If you're getting the idea I'm in favor of scrapping the wedding culture in America, you're right! Whether the wedding is a joyful peak experience or a total nightmare, either one can set your marriage up to fail.

Let's say you get the Ken and Barbie or Cinderella and Prince Charming fairytale wedding. All the planning went well. The families all got along.

The wedding day was amazing. The honeymoon was fabulous. You had the perfect dream wedding. (How many people do you know who got that result? But you will, right?)

After your perfect wedding, the honeymoon is over, and life happens. You have jobs, bills, dirty dishes, dirty laundry, a house or apartment to clean, groceries to buy, and all of the other parts of everyday life. And by the way, everybody isn't focused on you anymore. You're not the center of attention.

You may begin to wonder why every day of your marriage doesn't feel like your wedding day. You may begin to wonder what's wrong with your marriage or even if you made a mistake getting married. **Nothing is wrong with your marriage.** You're comparing everyday life to a once (hopefully) in a lifetime experience.

Another possible outcome is Murphy's Law applied, and everything about your wedding went wrong. Your families couldn't get along. Your mother or his mother made everyone miserable. No one respected your wishes or those of your spouse. People got drunk at the rehearsal dinner, came to the wedding drunk or hungover, or got trashed at the reception. You cried your eyes out, or your spouse got drunk to avoid the drama, and you were miserable. One or both of you passed out before the wedding night. Does that sound like a great start to a relationship that's supposed to last forever?

In the United States, many young girls are raised to be princesses. Their parents call them "princess" and teach them to want the fantasy wedding in the Disney movies. Here's the problem. A smart man doesn't want a princess. He wants a queen who will pick up a sword and fight at his side. He wants a partner, not someone he has to shelter from every challenge of life.

The existence of the television show *Bridezilla* drives me out of my mind. The title comes from *Godzilla*, a 1960s Japanese monster movie. Any suggestion the infantile behavior depicted on the show is acceptable is absurd. If you're adult enough to be married, you're adult enough to recognize other people have needs, desires, and wants, and it's not all about the bride. To the extent *Bridezilla* represents the wedding culture in America, I rest my case.

Finally, let's deal with one of the more dangerous traditions of the wedding culture: bachelor and bachelorette parties. Think for a moment about the message behind those parties. Far from being a celebration of the start of an amazing forever marriage, it's a funeral that says, "This is your last night of freedom before you start to wear the ball and chain." Why would any couple who love each other and are excited to be married even want to participate in something that denigrates the essential purpose of marriage?

And let's not forget most of those parties involve immense quantities of alcohol (or illicit, mood-altering substances) that reduce inhibitions, eliminate common sense, and involve a decidedly sexual orientation. How many marriages are destroyed by things that happen at those events? If the bride or groom have sex with someone else at the bachelor or bachelorette party, the marriage is over before it started.

What do you say to your marriage partner? "It didn't mean anything" or "I was drunk," or "I was high." Being drunk or high is not an excuse, it's an indictment of one's fitness to be married. They weren't adult enough to stay in control of their faculties to protect themselves, their spouse, and their marriage.

Most of you avoid walking through the bad part of your city or town alone at night, because you recognize that while you should be safe, it's still dangerous, and you don't take the risk. Use that same logic and assume bachelor and bachelorette parties are in the bad part of town.

This chapter is short for a reason. The more of the wedding culture you eliminate, the less stress you'll have, and the more focus you'll keep on the things that really matter, like building a firm foundation for your forever marriage.

Chapter 3

PLAN YOUR MARRIAGE

One reason so many marriages fail is couples spend an enormous amount of time, energy, and money planning a wedding, and spend no time planning the marriage. They failed to ask the questions we talked about in Chapter 1 before saying "I do." They fell into the trap of the wedding industry money machine we talked about in Chapter 2. But you're not going to make those mistakes.

You're going to use this simple formula to plan a forever marriage. No matter how much time, energy, and money you spend planning the wedding, spend ten times as much time, energy, and money planning your marriage. Imagine how the divorce statistics in America would change if every couple followed that formula?

Couples would start their marriage by building a firm foundation for a forever relationship. They would be building lasting, loving homes that would be safe places to raise children. They would be far less likely to divorce, because they worked through the hard questions together before they got married.

What does that look like? What do you really mean? First, spend time having those conversations about sex, money, children, and religion. Plan your marriage and your personal growth with guides like Brian Tracy, Tony Robbins, Dale Carnegie, Og Mandino, Stephen Covey, Brian Bouchard and many of the other authors listed on the reading list at the back of the book. Virtually all of them teach about the importance and power of setting goals.

Learn how to set goals for your marriage, your health, and your finances, and how to define the actions you'll need to take to achieve them. Learn how to make the daily commitments and actions necessary to develop the habits that drive you toward your goals. Understand that challenges will come. Will you complain about them or use them as fuel to motivate you to do more and be more?

Please take five minutes and watch Rocky Balboa's speech to his son at *www.youtube.com/watch?v=aLn7VQlPQOg*. For me, it's the single best part of all of the Rocky movies.

Starting a marriage without a plan is like starting a business without a business plan. According to the U.S. Small Business Administration, about two-thirds of new businesses with employees last two years, and about 50 percent last five years. See *www.sba.gov/sites/default/files/Business-Survival.pdf*.

If all investing time in a marriage plan did was increase your odds of having a forever marriage even a little, would it be worth it? If you think so, there's a Marriage Planning Form at the back of this book. Any time you invest in it will pay huge dividends.

How do you create a marriage plan? Start by describing what you believe would be an ideal day in your perfect married life. What time would you get up? Where would you be? What would you do each morning to set your day up for success? How would you feel when you woke up? How would you feel about your spouse when you woke up? How would you speak to them when you woke up? What would you have left for them to find later in the day to remind them how much you love and appreciate them? How grateful would you be to walk through life's journey with them?

Marriage is the most important partnership you'll ever form, whether you're an employee, a business owner, a teacher, fireman, or policeman. The most sacred contract you'll ever make is with the person you marry. A wise friend of mine from many years ago said, "A man or woman who will cheat on their spouse will cheat you in business." He was exactly right.

If a person thinks so little of the sacred obligation of fidelity they made to the man or woman they married and promised to spend their life with, why would any business partner believe that person won't cheat them? Infidelity reveals character, maturity, and the ability to make and keep commitments.

I'm not saying every marriage will be perfect. I'm not even saying every marriage should last forever. I am saying a forever marriage requires complete physical and emotional fidelity. Part of your Marriage Plan is how each of you define complete fidelity and what role pornography plays in your definition.

Men, a word to the wise. Many of the women I've worked with over the years define their husband viewing pornography as infidelity. It creates insecurity about your feelings for them, magnifies the body image issues our society has instilled in them, and leaves them feeling rejected or as though they are not enough for you. None of those feelings strengthens the love, joy, passion, and connection between the two of you, or contributes to building a forever marriage.

For me, complete physical and emotional fidelity means you don't flirt with the cute guy or cute girl at work, at school, where you volunteer, in your church, or anywhere else. You don't participate in any activity that could allow emotional attachments to form. You don't carry on long phone, email, or text conversations with anyone that could lead to emotional attachment.

If you're married, your ex-boyfriends and ex-girlfriends are off limits. "We're just friends" is nonsense. Some religions use the acronym WWJD to help people make decisions (What would Jesus do?). In secular terms, don't have a conversation with anyone unless you'd be completely comfortable copying your husband or wife. If there's any conversation you need to have with anyone (especially an ex-boyfriend or ex-girlfriend) you wouldn't want your spouse to see or hear, you shouldn't have that conversation.

Bringing children to the marriage requires one or both of you to deal with the children's other biological parent. It's necessary, but rarely fun. Even in that situation, be careful. Don't meet with your ex-wife or ex-husband in your home unless your new spouse is there, or in their home unless another adult is present.

Many divorce lawyers would tell you to only meet with your ex-spouse in a public place, so you can't be accused of attacking them. Both men and women make unfounded allegations of assault to gain an advantage in the divorce or child custody dispute, or just out of spite.

What else do you plan about your marriage? Go beyond just looking at a perfect day. Where do you plan to be as a couple physically, emotionally, financially, geographically, and educationally in one year? What about five, ten, twenty and thirty years from now? What about when you retire, whether that's ten years or fifty years from now?

What do you want your marriage to look like at each of those intervals? What's your plan to get there? How are you going to measure success? What goals do you need to achieve to make your dream marriage a reality? What's your plan to achieve those goals? What actions do you need to take now and in the future to achieve them? What actions are you going to take each day? What action are you going to take **right now** to create excitement and momentum to propel you forward and motivate you?

If you don't have a plan, none of it is likely to happen. Things are going to happen along the way to knock you off course. A plan you both agree on and are committed to makes you far better able to weather the storm and get back on course. Does that mean you're going to design your entire life when you're 18 or 25 or 30 years old and get married for the first time? You can, but that doesn't mean your plan isn't going to change.

An airline pilot will tell you if they're flying from JFK airport in New York to LAX airport in Los Angeles they're off course 90+ percent of the time, due to factors affecting air travel like wind direction and velocity.

The airliner gets from JFK to LAX and lands safely because the plane and the pilots constantly make small course corrections. If the wind moves them a little bit off course, they immediately make the necessary correction and keep moving toward their destination.

Pilots don't wait to make corrections until they've been flying at 400 mph for six hours. A one-degree error from JFK to LAX means you're 50 miles off course. If you're five degrees off course for 3,000 miles, you're 300 miles from your destination. The formula is distance off track = (number of degrees off course x distance to destination)/60. In simple terms, the farther you are off course and the farther you travel, the farther from your destination you'll be.

Marriages are measured in time, not distance, so in marriage, the formula means small uncorrected errors get magnified the longer the marriage lasts. If you're a little off course now and don't make a correction, in ten, twenty, or thirty years, you'll be far from your intended destination. If you have a common goal and common direction, and you're constantly focused on where you want to end up together, you're much more likely to arrive at a Diamond Marriage; one that stands the test of time.

Step back and look and say, "Let me make the small course correction necessary to get me or our marriage back on track toward that long-term goal we set five, ten, twenty, or thirty years ago." When you consistently make little course corrections, getting to the destination is much easier. Some of those course corrections might include biting your tongue when that critical comment is about to slip out of your mouth and being willing to say I'm sorry, even if you don't think you were wrong.

Step 1 is being joyful together. Step 2 is being grateful every day when you wake up and look over at the man or woman lying next to you. You give thanks for the gift of another day with this person. Before you lay down at night, give thanks for the day and tell them, "I can't imagine spending a day without you. Thank you for this day."

What would it be worth to feel total love, joy, passion, and connection with your spouse every day? What would your life be like? You can have it. You just have to make a plan and do the work. Everything you ever have in life that's worthwhile requires work and sacrifice.

Commit to making your Marriage Plan. Adjust your plan to make sure you're on target to get to your dream marriage. How many couples do you know who sat down before they got married and wrote out a plan for their married life? None of the ones who were divorced did, and a great percentage of the ones who stayed married didn't either. Maybe the ones who stayed happily married were more committed. Maybe they asked themselves and their spouse better questions. Maybe their communication was a little better. Maybe they just got lucky.

What do you think would happen to the divorce statistics in America if every couple put together a written plan for their marriage before they got married? If you go to a bank to get a business loan, the banker will ask to see your business plan and financials. They want to know your plan to gauge the risk of loaning you money. How are you going to execute your plan? How are you going to use the money you want to borrow?

In today's culture, if you ask a couple about to be married to explain their plan, their answer almost certainly would be about the wedding plans. What would happen if the pastor, counselor, or minister stopped them and said, "I'm not interested in the wedding plan. What's your plan for your marriage? I want to see a written plan. I want to know where you're going to be a year from now, five years from now, ten years from now, twenty years from now, when you retire. What do you want your ideal marriage to look like? How are you going to raise children? What are you going to do financially? Where are you going to live? What are you going to do for your education? Are you going to own businesses or get jobs? What kind of jobs?"

Can you imagine the stunned look on the couple's faces? That look demonstrates the failure of the wedding culture to prepare couples for marriage. Those questions force you to think through what you're about to do and how you're going to make it successful. They prepare you for the bumps in the road of life.

Your Marriage Plan is a blueprint for your forever marriage. Now it's time to live your plan.

Chapter 4

The Honeymoon is Over - NOW WHAT?

Your wedding was a wonderful, peak experience. Or it was a complete disaster. Or something in the middle. The honeymoon's over. Now what happens? If one or both of you are still in college, you may go back to school on a full-time basis with the obligations and time commitments that go along with completing your education. One or both of you may have to go back to your jobs.

The time leading up to your wedding was totally focused on you and was filled with bridal showers, bachelorette and bachelor parties and wedding preparation, (unless you followed the advice in this book). Either way, the focus is not on you anymore. You're not the center of attention. The world requires you to focus on your education, your employer, and your spouse.

Then everyday life happens—things like buying groceries, dropping off the laundry, picking up the laundry, doing the laundry at home, doing the dishes, doing the cooking, cleaning the house, and taking care of the car(s). All the parts of daily life that get ignored in the runup to the wedding come back with added weight. You begin to wonder why things don't feel like they did when you got married. You may think, *This doesn't feel like my wedding day.*

It's not supposed to. Your wedding was an event. Your marriage is a living organism that grows or dies a little each day, depending on the choices you and your spouse make that day.

If you planned the marriage, instead of spending all your time, energy, and money planning the wedding, the marriage will be better now that you don't have the distractions of other people and their agendas or calendars. You get back to running your own life and living it the way you planned. You begin to develop habits that bind you together and grow and deepen the love and connection between you.

It's the little things you do every day. Many of those little things revolve around commitment to each other and your own level of emotional growth and development. The television show *Bridezilla* depicts a very low level of emotional growth and glamorizes a purely selfish, narcissistic view, where life is all about the bride. It's really a continuation of the teenage mindset, where the entire universe revolves around you and your needs.

A higher level of emotional growth and development allows you to act selflessly. That doesn't mean ignoring your own needs, but it does mean having the ability to put your partner's needs ahead of yours at times. It means being able to have an adult conversation about how to work together to meet as many of each of your needs as possible.

A my-way-or-the-highway attitude is the highway to divorce court. Many people walk that highway more than once and never figure out they set out on the highway to divorce the day they got married. They haven't developed the ability to recognize that different people attach different levels of importance to every issue. For example, if something is vitally important to your spouse, and less important to you, give on that one.

When you're negotiating a business or real estate deal, or you're trying to negotiate a settlement of a dispute or a lawsuit, you're trying to find a creative solution that gives each party as much of what they want and need as possible. At times, it's also about allowing the other side (your spouse) to save face.

Two people who are selfless in the sense they put the interests of the other first will have a joyful marriage. A wonderful short story called, "A Special Christmas Story: The Gift of the Magi" by O. Henry is about a young married couple. The woman had long beautiful hair. Her husband had inherited his grandfather's pocket watch. They had no money to buy Christmas presents for each other.

The young man sold his grandfather's pocket watch to buy a set of combs made of shells with jewels at the edge for his wife's beautiful hair. The young woman had sold her beautiful hair to buy a silver chain for his gold pocket watch. She no longer had the beautiful hair. He no longer had the gold pocket watch. But they had a loving relationship and a story that has been told over and over for more than 100 years.

Planning your marriage doesn't end with the wedding. It includes sitting down regularly and counseling together as a couple to make sure you both feel like you're on track and to make whatever adjustments need to be made. It doesn't matter whether you call it a family meeting or family council. Here's what it looks like.

Set aside time on a regular basis, perhaps weekly—certainly at least monthly—when you eliminate all distractions. It's not done in a restaurant, where you're being interrupted by the waiter or waitress and trying to talk over the din of the crowd or the clang of pots and pans.

It's a quiet time in a quiet place, where you've turned off all electronic devices. No cell phone, no laptop or tablet, no TV, no music, no nothing. You give each other the gift of your full attention and communicate honestly. Remember the principle of brutal honesty with yourself and gentle honesty with your spouse.

If you do that meeting weekly, it's also a great time to plan your week. Make sure you block out time together as a couple, and when children come along, family time. Many of us do a great job of keeping calendars and a lousy job of calendaring the important things. Your family comes first. Plan your calendar that way. Treat family time as important and sacred. Once you've put family time in your calendars, then schedule your classes, your jobs, and whatever else you're doing.

Keep a record of your family meetings or councils either in a journal or electronically so you can refer back to them. You don't always need to know where you came from to get to a destination, but sometimes, when you look back, you gain perspective on the course corrections needed to get you to the right destination. Don't forget to celebrate when you arrive at one of those destinations or hit one of the interim milestones. Enjoy the journey.

Set aside a time one night a week and do something together. We call it date night. You and your spouse go out together with no children, no phones, no distractions, and just spend time with each other. It doesn't have to be fancy or expensive. It doesn't have to cost anything. Date night can be making a sack lunch, walking to the local park, sitting down and eating and talking together, and walking back together, holding hands. Have fun. Be creative. Use that time to reconnect with each other every week.

Date night is even more important when children come along. It may be difficult to leave an infant at all for the first few weeks, but don't let that pattern continue for long. Even if the mother is nursing, she can pump and leave enough milk for an hour or two away.

Hopefully, you'll have friends or family who can watch your child for a couple of hours to give you a break, because you're going to need it. It doesn't matter if date night is the same night every week, just get it on the calendar every week, and make it happen.

Let me share our personal story about date night. I had heard about date night for over ten years, but I was busy. I had a busy law practice and was busy in church responsibilities and coaching kids' baseball and soccer. Linda and I were a taxi service for three busy kids. Date night just never got on the calendar. Finally, I'd heard enough about date night to give it a try.

We picked Friday night, and we made it out two Friday nights in a row. By Tuesday or Wednesday of the third week, Linda asked me, "What are we doing for date night?" At that moment, I realized how important it was to her. She got my undivided attention for a couple of hours when I wasn't distracted by work, TV, church, or children.

I got the same benefit. I got her full attention. She was incredibly busy taking care of me, our three children, and our home. During date night, she wasn't distracted by all the things she did to take care of our family.

I wouldn't have changed jobs with her for anything in the world. She worked harder inside the home than I ever did anywhere else.

Date night changed our marriage for the better, and we continue to do it weekly. Sometimes, we can't do it on Friday night. If we have a grandchild's concert or soccer game on Friday night, we adjust. We find a different night and go out to eat. I used to ask Linda if she wanted to go to a movie for date night. Her answer emphasized the importance of date night. She said, "No, because we don't get to talk at movies."

Date night isn't common practice yet, but maybe this book will help. When you do date night on a consistent basis, you stoke the flame between you that can burn for a lifetime. You may find you married your best friend, and they will forever be your confidant, your lover, the keeper of your secrets, the holder of your heart. A forever marriage should be joyful. You're getting to spend your life with the person you'd rather be with than anyone else in the world.

We all make mistakes. If you think you're perfect and your partner is the problem; you're already wrong and just proved you're not perfect. Would your relationship work better if you both start with the assumption, "I'm going to make some mistakes in this relationship, so I'm going to want and need tolerance and forgiveness from my spouse." For you to expect tolerance and forgiveness from your spouse, you must be tolerant and forgiving. We're not talking about infidelity.

It's the little things--little things that may matter a great deal to you and not so much to your spouse, or vice versa. Things may be very important to your spouse and not very important to you. If your spouse is a sports fanatic, they may want to watch their favorite team play. It's important to them, but you don't like sports. No problem. You don't have to watch the game with them (but if you don't, you shouldn't expect them to go to the movie you want to see). If you want your spouse to do things with you they don't enjoy, it has to be a two-way street.

Being considerate means you don't plan a couples' outing when you know their ballgame is going to be on. It also means you care enough about your spouse's wants and needs to find out when the game is on before you plan a conflicting activity. That approach meets as many of both of your needs as possible. You're not going to have 100 percent of your needs met 100 percent of the time. If you walk through life side-by-side and hand-in-hand, each giving a little, you both get the love, joy, passion, and connection that can be part of a forever marriage.

Your spouse is not a child and will not respond well to being treated like one. You married an adult who has wants, needs, desires, and plans of their own. For your marriage to last forever, both of you will need to compromise. Women rightly rejected the male-dominated culture of the 1950s where the "little woman" stayed barefoot, pregnant, in the kitchen, and was expected to be seen and not heard.

Since the 1950s, American culture has evolved to the point some women believe they should be so totally independent that, "No man will ever tell me what to do about anything—and if he doesn't like it, he can get out." Just as women rejected male domination, any man worth having will reject being dominated by a woman. Lasting, loving marriages happen when both parties are mature enough to compromise.

Some of those compromises can be based on the strength of your respective feelings about issues where there's conflict. If you had the sex, money, children and religion conversations before you said I do, you probably identified at least some of each of your core values.

Core values are the things you absolutely must have in order to be happy and fulfilled in your marriage and things you absolutely cannot tolerate and still be happy and fulfilled in the marriage. The time to find out what those are and to make sure yours and your spouses are not in direct conflict is before you say "I do." Remember, if even one of your core values directly conflicts with one of your spouse's core values, you're fundamentally incompatible, and the likelihood of a lasting, loving marriage is very slim.

Go back to the example of a woman who feels she must be a mother to be fulfilled. Having children is one of her core values. If her husband feels that he must not bring a child into today's world and is adamantly opposed to having children for that reason, not having children is one of his core values. That man and woman are fundamentally incompatible, because who they are at their core and what they need as human beings directly conflicts. Compromise on a core value doesn't work.

If the woman agrees not to have children to be with the man, over time as she attends baby showers, watches her friends, colleagues, and co-workers have babies, listens to others talk about their children, and feels her biological clock ticking, she will regret that decision. She may go into the marriage thinking her man will change his mind and bring up having a child from time to time. Each time he rejects her request because it conflicts with one of his core values, she will feel a deeper wound, a greater longing.

She may even decide to take matters into her own hands and stop taking birth control pills and get pregnant without his knowledge or consent. That betrayal almost inevitably will be fatal to the marriage because she shattered the pillar of trust his love for her rests on. If not having children is one of his core values, he will see her getting pregnant without his consent as the ultimate betrayal, and the end of that marriage is coming. And the child suffers the consequences of the divorce.

The circumstances can be reversed. The man may feel a biological imperative to procreate; to leave a legacy. His dream may even have been to have a large family. If his wife agrees to that before the marriage and then changes her mind (or wasn't honest about her core value of not having children), he will feel betrayed at a deep level.

In either situation, the spouse whose core value has been rejected will feel pain, withdrawal, rejection, and, ultimately, nothing at all for their spouse. At that point, the marriage is effectively dead, and it's time to pull the plug. Asking the "Before You Say I Do" questions helps avoid this marriage disaster.

Once you've identified your core values, (the must-haves and can't tolerates), and learned those are not conflicting, look at the other things on each of your lists. Those are the should-haves and the don't likes. They will vary in importance, and their relative importance should be reflected in the compromises you each make to create a lasting, loving marriage.

A couple of examples may help illustrate this principle. If religion (or religious practice in the home) is critically important to one partner and not very important to the other partner, the religious compromises may need to be shaded in the direction of the spouse for whom it is a critical value.

Allowing religious practice and supporting your spouse in it are totally different concepts. Most of the work I've done with couples has been faith-based where one spouse is active in their faith and the other isn't active or isn't even a member of their spouse's faith.

If you go into marriage knowing religious practice is one of your spouse's core values, you need to be prepared to allow religious practice in the home and to support religious practice by your children. Since it's a core value, the commitment you make is a lifelong commitment, and changing your mind is a fundamental betrayal of trust that will damage the marriage—perhaps irreversibly.

If one spouse feels very strongly about time at home and the other partner tends to be more social and wants to go out or have others over all the time, have an honest discussion about how strongly you each feel about that issue, and keep in mind that if she compromised more on one issue, he needs to give more on the other one.

If the marriage is going to be lasting and loving, there is no room for physical or emotional infidelity.

According to the U.S. Social Security Administration's 2015 actuarial table (the last one available online on 12/8/18), if you marry at age 20, you can expect to be married for 57 years (yes, the man is likely to die first). Imagine the changes you'll experience in the world around you and in your marriage. A man who is currently 77 years old was born in 1941, around the time the Japanese bombed Pearl Harbor and the United States entered World War II.

Think about the profound changes in his world. The first public demonstration of television was in 1934. In 1941, few U.S. homes had television. Some had large, tube-based radios. Some still had no radio or TV. He's seen black-and-white televisions, color televisions, and now multiple flat-screen televisions in many homes, color cameras, disposable cameras, commercial jet airliners, eight-track tapes (Google it), cassette tapes, VHS tapes, DVD and BlueRay players, the invention of desktop computers, floppy discs, hard discs, CDs, DVDs, external hard drives, cell phones, men on the moon, the space shuttle, and hundreds of 24-hour TV channels.

Did you know that in the 1960s, there were only three TV stations: ABC, NBC, and CBS, and depending on where you lived, you could usually only pick up two of them? Did you know they went off the air at midnight?

If you're 20 years old today, take a few minutes and think about how things have changed in your lifetime, and about things you take for granted that didn't exist when you were born. Changes on that same scale are going to take place in a marriage that lasts 50 years. If you start out with your core values aligned and a plan for your marriage, you're much better equipped to navigate the rocks and shoals of life.

Linda and I got married at 17 and 18 years old. Over the last 42 years, we've gone through a staggering number of changes. We've grown up together. Changes and challenges that could have broken us bonded us more closely together. Today, there's nothing I enjoy more than just being with her. If I'm working in our home office, I just want to know she's in the house.

We're blessed that several of our grandchildren live in the area. Linda drives them to and from school many days. Even though they're 14, 12 and 10, every day when they come into our home, they want to know if Papa (me) is there. They don't need to come in the office to see me. They just need to know I'm there.

Linda and I are part of their security. You're part of your children's security. Unless they live in an abusive home, children just want to know mom and dad are there. Maybe that's one of the reasons why divorce is so devastating to children. It's also a great reason to do everything in your power to provide a loving, stable home for your children and a model for the relationship you want them to have with their spouse.

Whether they know it or not, every father models for his daughters how they should expect to be treated by their husbands, and models for his sons what kind of men and husbands they should be and how they should treat their wives. Every mother models for her sons how they should expect to be treated by their wives, and models for her daughters what kind of wives and mothers they should be and how they should treat their husbands.

Whether you already have children or plan to have children, take a moment to write in the space below the examples you and your spouse are currently setting for your children, and the examples you're committed to setting for them from today forward. Ask your spouse to prepare the same list. Then, compare, discuss, and begin living your new commitments today.

As you go through your daily married life, you're going to have days when you don't feel as good as normal. That's one of those times when personal development literature can be a great help. You can learn to focus on positive things to help you manage the way you feel. Begin by accepting 100 percent responsibility for your own happiness.

Happiness is a choice, not the result of what other people do or say or don't do or say. ***No one makes you feel anything.*** You choose how to feel in response to what they say or do or fail to say or do. The time between their actions and your feelings is a space called "choice." Your spouse chose what to say or do, and you chose how to feel in response. Your spouse is responsible for their choices, and you're responsible for yours.

I told each of my sons to marry a sunshine girl. Each of them asked me to explain what I meant. A sunshine girl is happy and has a smile on her face when she opens her eyes in the morning and realizes she's still alive. Life with her will be joyful.

Someone who constantly looks for and expects the best of people and situations will get what they expect most of the time. People who expect the worst of people and situations also will get what they expect most of the time, will be miserable, and will make everyone around them miserable. And nothing their husband or wife does "to make them happy" will ever be enough.

After reading this book, you have a choice of how you want to approach life and what kind of partner and parent you want to be. Write in the space below - What kind of person will you be? What kind of people do you want your children to be?

_____
_____
_____
_____
_____
_____
_____
_____
_____
_____
_____
_____

Grandparents have a special place in their hearts for their grandchildren. They think their grandchildren are the smartest, most talented, best-looking grandchildren in the world. (They're wrong, mine are, but that's another story). The point is, your children will be the parents of your grandchildren. If you knew today your children would parent exactly how you parent them, what would you change? Write your answers in the space below.

I recently met with a man whose wife had been unfaithful. He believed it was a one-time event and wanted to save the marriage. He said his wife claimed to want to repair the marriage and was sorry for what she'd done. He told me his wife owned her cheating 100 percent.

I asked him to explain to me what she says about why she cheated. He began by saying, "she said that I—" and I stopped him. When she began to explain why she cheated by talking about him, she clearly had not taken full responsibility for her actions. She doesn't own the cheating. She still wants to blame him or use him as an excuse.

He didn't tell her to take off her clothes and get in bed with another man. She chose to do that, and nothing he did **made** her do those things. She chose to, and until she's adult enough and humble enough to accept that she is 100 percent responsible for the infidelity and has the responsibility to repair the damage done, "there is nothing to fix." He leaned back in his chair and said, "I wish she had heard you say that."

He described how for their entire marriage, her parents and family had given him a very hard time about things he hadn't done, and she had never once stood up to her family to defend him. She has a great deal of growing up to do for that marriage to survive. It could just as easily have been the man who cheated. If he explains to his wife why he cheated and talks about her, he doesn't own it yet, and they can't fix it till he owns it.

Infidelity is one of the most difficult challenges in marriage to overcome. When you decided to get married, you made a decision to be together forever. Traditional wedding vows usually include phrases like, "for better or worse, for richer or poorer, in sickness and health, and forsaking all others."

You make that promise in front of friends, family, and some officiant, and the first time things go bad, you want to run for the hills. Maybe that's because we live in an immediate gratification and disposable society. We want it all, we want it now, and we want everything to be perfect. Life doesn't work that way. The road will be rocky.

If you've ever exercised, there have been days you didn't want to get out of bed. You didn't want to put on your workout clothes. You didn't want to put on your tennis shoes. You didn't want to open the door to go out and run or go to the gym, but you did it anyway. That workout strengthened you physically and mentally. Mentally, because you kept your commitment to yourself and put yourself one day closer to having a lifelong habit. Physically, because you feel so good for doing what your body needed.

Emotions work the same way. You grow emotionally when you don't want to reach out or be vulnerable, when you're afraid to be hurt, and you make the choice to be vulnerable and go for it. To be married forever and have joy in your marriage, you must risk being hurt. You must be vulnerable.

No emotional vulnerability means no love, no passion and no connection. If one or both of you are so afraid of being hurt or abandoned or abused or cheated on that they won't allow themselves to feel pain anymore, they can't feel joy either. To have joy requires you to risk being hurt.

We create our own rules for when we allow ourselves to feel love, joy, passion, and connection. And we can change those rules in an instant if we know the secret and apply it. Some people create such complicated rules for being joyful it's almost impossible for them to feel joy.

If your rules for being joyful are your spouse must never think or say anything negative about you, must anticipate and fulfill your every need, want, and desire without asking you, and must do what you want them to do all the time, how often will you feel joy? Unless you're living with someone I haven't met, the answer is never! Worst of all, you have no control over the other person, so you've given someone else power to decide how you feel. Why would you do that?

What would happen if you changed your rules, so you would feel joy every time you thought of, saw, heard, or touched your spouse? Now who's in control of your feelings? You are! And those rules are so simple, you'll feel joy every day. You also can also do fun and thoughtful things for your spouse to spice up their lives and make them feel loved and appreciated. When you help them feel joyful, they become your raving fans. Why would your spouse cheat on someone who helps them feel amazing?

Love requires you to risk being hurt, but it's worth it. You can build a loving marriage and enjoy every minute with your spouse. Love at home makes everything else in life fixable or bearable. It doesn't really matter how much money you have or how great things go in your business or career. If you're miserable in your relationship, you're miserable.

Chapter 5

YOUR FIRST BABY CHANGES EVERYTHING

Pregnancy is amazing and terrifying. A tiny little baby bump grows until she feels the first little flutter kick, and then you put your hand on her stomach and feel your baby move. For a man, that evokes powerful emotional feelings. I can't even imagine what it feels like for a woman physically or emotionally - I've never experienced it from that perspective.

For me (and for many men) there is something special about a pregnant woman, something beautiful and miraculous. Part of your job as a man and husband is to make your wife feel beautiful and remind her how beautiful she is every single day.

A pregnant woman's body goes through incredible changes. Her hormone levels, appetite, energy level, and comfort level change minute to minute. As pregnancy progresses, she struggles to find any comfortable position day or night. Sleep may be almost impossible. Even her breathing gets more difficult. As her center of gravity changes and she has to wear different clothes, she isn't comfortable and probably doesn't feel beautiful or sexy.

Is pregnancy ever without challenges? No. Sometimes the hormonal changes women experience result in anger, tears, wild swings of emotion, morning sickness, afternoon sickness, evening sickness, night sickness, irritability, inability to sleep, and a lack of interest in sex. Pregnancy can challenge any marriage.

Remember the principles of honest communication about what each of you are thinking and feeling. But men, please make sure you're not within arm's reach if you expect an honest answer to, "How are you feeling?" Sometimes, the best thing you can do is just hold her and tell her you love her. Sometimes, just leave her alone. You're going to have to figure that one out, because every woman is unique and special.

Until your first baby is born, you can pick up and go when and where you want. During pregnancy, you can still go out without advance planning, though at some point in the pregnancy, she may not be able to venture too far from a bathroom. You don't need a diaper bag, stroller, sippy cup (if you don't know what those are, you will), or bags of Cheerios. There's nothing to take with you. It's still pick-up-and-go just as you've always done.

Everything changes when she says, "I'm in labor! Take me to the hospital." Hopefully, you've gone through parenting classes and birthing classes and have toured the hospital where your wife plans to deliver, so you have some understanding about what's going to happen. If you've done those things, it will reduce your anxiety—at least slightly.

Pack a suitcase a couple of weeks before her due date and put it in the car and leave it. You don't know when you're going to need it, and you may not remember it when her water breaks at 3:00 in the morning and she says, "We have to go now!" She's going to say *now* in a way that will make absolutely clear to you if your feet aren't on the floor in ten seconds, you may be a dead man.

Even when you do all that planning and preparation, your birth plan is likely to go out the window-- especially if it's your first baby. You'll be lucky to get your pants on and zipped to go out the front door. If the suitcase is already in the car, you eliminated one of the things you could forget.

I read a story on Facebook about the funniest things nurses have seen happen during birth. One nurse told about a man who ran into the emergency room saying, "My wife's getting ready to deliver!" The nurse said, "Well, where's your wife?" He forgot his wife and had to go home and get her. I don't know if the story is true, but it illustrates the anxiety level labor can create. Everyone reacts to stress differently.

It's critically important for the husband and wife to agree upon who will be in the delivery room before they tell anyone, including family members, they're pregnant. Remember the lesson about discussing the wedding before telling anyone you're engaged? Most hospitals in the U.S. allow the husband and one or two others to be in the delivery room. Some are even more relaxed about who is in the delivery room.

Most couples are probably better off deciding *no one* will be in the delivery room except the two of them, especially if it's their first child. Everyone else can wait outside. The birth of a child is an incredibly intimate moment for a couple. They need to bond with their baby and strengthen their bond with each other. Anyone other than the husband or wife in the delivery room adds a level of uncertainty, anxiety, and complexity that, in most situations—particularly with first births—isn't worth the extra aggravation.

The couple should have as much control over the birth as possible under the circumstances, and both families should respect their wishes without question. No matter what decision they make about who will be in the delivery room, the couple must be absolutely unified when their decision is presented to their families.

If you think you want to invite others into the delivery room, please take time (seven or eight months) to rethink that decision before you tell anyone they can be in the delivery room. If someone raises the topic or assumes they'll be in the delivery room, gently but firmly correct them immediately and say something like, "We haven't decided if anyone else will be in the delivery room and won't until much closer to delivery." That buys you lots of time to make a decision. And remember, **no one** other than the two of you have any *right* to be in the delivery room.

In the 1950s and 60s, even fathers weren't allowed in the delivery room. Dad was pacing in the waiting room along with everyone else. In the 1970s, hospitals began allowing fathers to be in the delivery room for normal births, but not for C-sections. By the 1980s, even that restriction disappeared.

Our first child was born at Jackson Hospital in Montgomery, Alabama, in 1977. Linda got the second ultrasound examination her obstetrician had ever done. He got the machine the day of her appointment. We sat in the waiting room with another young couple who lived in a small mobile home. The young man had a half-cast on his arm that covered multiple stitches. He worked at a grocery store and had gotten seriously cut with a box cutter while stocking shelves.

The other couple went in first, and the young man came out about 15 minutes later, white as a sheet saying, "There's two of them. There's two of them. What are we going to do?" I told Linda we were leaving. We didn't, and thankfully, we only had one!

When she went into labor, I was one of the first father's in the delivery room in that hospital. They put me in scrubs and sat me on a stool by Linda's head and assigned a nurse to watch me. The nurses were so afraid a father in the delivery room would be a disaster. Watching my baby come out was the most fascinating thing I'd ever seen in my life. When the doctor finished cutting the umbilical cord, he wrapped our son in a blanket and handed him to me.

When he handed our son to me, powerful feelings of love and responsibility washed over me. I loved him instantly and knew I would do anything to protect him. Those feelings never changed. I had those same feelings when each of our other two children were handed to me. They changed my life. I was grateful to Linda for giving me each child and knew my job for the rest of my life was to take care of them.

After a particularly difficult and painful delivery, the nurse handed our daughter to me. I said, "Wow, that didn't hurt a bit." (Not one of my finest moments). Fortunately, I was across the room holding our daughter, so Linda couldn't throw anything at me, but if looks could kill, our marriage would have ended at five years.

Deliveries have changed dramatically in the last 40 years. Instead of delivering in an operating room, many hospital birthing centers look like hotel rooms. No one has to wear gowns or masks. It feels much more relaxed and much less rigid. The woman has much more control over the experience.

The birth is over. You're a new mom or dad. You're still in the hospital getting no sleep, and now are taking care of a newborn baby. For those of you with no experience, that means cleaning the umbilical cord, feeding, holding and bathing the baby, and changing tiny diapers containing some of the worst smells in the world. And, yet, there is absolutely nothing more special and miraculous than holding your newborn child.

Then, you get to go home. You came into the hospital with a very pregnant wife and maybe one little suitcase. You leave the hospital with a not-pregnant wife, a newborn baby, a diaper bag, a car seat, and a load of other stuff you need for this tiny little person. We took our son home in a 1969 Volkswagen Beetle with an automatic clutch and "air conditioning" (the running boards were so rusted outside air came in through the body). We traded it before winter, because it was too cold to carry an infant.

After we took our son home, every time we wanted to go somewhere, we had to have a car seat, a stroller, a diaper bag, formula, bottles, wipes, and even little bags to put diapers into. It wasn't pick-up-and-go anymore. Every trip to the grocery store became an adventure. By the time we got all the stuff we needed for the baby in a Volkswagen Beetle, we barely had room for groceries, which was fine, because with a new baby, we barely had money for groceries. Your baby changes your focus, because you now have a tiny human to protect who is completely dependent on you for everything, both physically and emotionally.

We've already talked about children being born master manipulators of adult behavior. Remember the sleepless nights when your baby was fed, burped, dry, and healthy? You rocked them to sleep, and as soon as you laid them down, they started to cry. What did you do? You picked them up, and they went back to sleep. And you did it over and over and over again until they woke up in the morning hungry, and you were too exhausted to keep your eyes open. They wanted to be held, they cried, and they got what they wanted.

Having a baby may change the parents' priorities in unhealthy ways. If you're a person of faith, your priorities should be first, your relationship with your creator, second, your spouse, third, your children, and fourth, everyone and everything else, including parents, in-laws, brothers, sisters, aunts, uncles, nieces, nephews, friends, hobbies (you get the idea). If you're not a person of faith, move the others up one position.

Unfortunately, many women place their children before their husband. A man who is faithful to his wife can only appropriately get affection and attention from her. If she's so focused on a child or children she doesn't provide him with the affection and attention he needs, by the time the last child leaves home, so will he. Or somewhere along the way, he will find someone else who puts him first. I am not condoning or excusing infidelity in any way, shape, or form. There is no excuse for infidelity, but if you know the problem, why wouldn't you address it?

The Old and New Testaments contain the same order of priority. Put the Lord your God first. Then, cleave to your husband or wife, and become one flesh. There is no commandment to cleave unto your children to the exclusion of your spouse. It doesn't work.

Think about the couple with three children born three years apart. They have a six-year-old, a three-year-old, and a newborn. By the time the newborn is 18 and out of the house (you hope), the oldest child is 24. The husband has been his wife's third, fourth, or fifth priority for a quarter of a century.

After 25 years of being low man on the totem pole (literally), do you really think there's a possibility of a fulfilling or satisfying relationship with his wife? Even though a baby changes logistics, it shouldn't change your priorities. Putting your spouse before your children helps create a forever marriage.

Children feel more secure knowing their parents place each other before them. It also teaches them what to expect from their own marriages. The idea may be easier to understand viewed as a function of time. If you marry at 25 and live a normal lifespan, you'll be married and living with your spouse for 50 years. Each child will live with you for 18 years (you hope). Why should you place the shorter relationship before the one that's supposed to last forever? The short answer is you can't have a forever marriage if you do.

What else does a child change? Everything! It changes the types of things you're able to do as a family. You're not going to take a six-month-old infant to a rock concert—or at least please don't. Linda I went to an outdoor concert at Blossom Music Center near Cleveland, Ohio when she was eight months pregnant with our second child. We loved the

Doobie Brothers (it was 1981, after all), but the music was loud, and our daughter, who was still in Linda's stomach, freaked out and wouldn't stop doing in-womb gymnastics. We left immediately.

You learn about caring for an infant and become the most important teachers your children will ever have. You decide what's going to be taught and who's going to teach. Do you have the option for one of you to be a stay-at-home parent, or will you need to put your child in daycare? Today's current economic situation requires many married couples to be two-income families. Financial pressures are even greater on a single parent, and no parent should feel guilty about putting their child in daycare.

When our first child was born, I was in college full-time and working two jobs. I worked midnight to 8:00 a.m. in a garbage bag factory as a machine operator, went home for breakfast and a shower, worked from 9:00 a.m. to noon for my Dad's civil engineering company, went to college from 1:00 - 5:00 p.m., went home to have dinner with my wife, see my new baby, went to bed at 7:00 p.m., got up at 11:00 p.m., and did it all over again. That was not the most fun period of my life.

Linda went back to work full time when our son was six or eight weeks old. My mom babysat our son for about six months, until caring for an infant wore her out, and we found a full-time sitter. Linda took off about a year after our second child was born. When she went back to work, our son and daughter were in daycare. When our third child was born, she stayed home because we couldn't afford the cost of daycare for three children. Our youngest son was with Linda all the time until he started pre-school. To this day, they have a special bond, probably because he spent so much more time with his mom.

Based on our personal experience, if it's possible for one spouse to stay home with a child, even if they work at a home-based business, it's worth the effort and the sacrifice. Even if you decide not to stay home, try to build a budget on one spouse's income, and save or invest the rest.

One of the educational questions is whether to teach your child a second language and when? A number of sources suggest that the earlier you teach a child a second language, the better. See *www.parents.com/toddlers-preschoolers/development/language/bilingual-babes-teach-your-child-a-second-language/*

"Studies by Harvard University confirm that the creativity, critical thinking skills, and flexibility of the mind are significantly enhanced if children learn a second language at a younger age. Preschool years—especially the first three years of life—are believed to be a vital period in a child's life. This is when the foundations for attitudes, thinking, and learning, among others, are laid down. . . . Using that ability is much encouraged because, always according to research, learning a second language is as easy as learning the first." *www.mother.ly/parenting/the-best-age-for-kids-to-learn-a-second-language*

That's a great gift to give your children. With so many multicultural families in America, it's wonderful children are able to speak multiple languages. If possible, teach your children at least two languages.

You have other educational decisions to make. Do you homeschool? Public or private school? Who takes care of the children after school? All of those are important decisions you should have discussed when you made your marriage plan. What are we going to do when children come along? How many do we want to have? How are we going to raise them?

How are we going to educate them? Is one of us going to stay home? Who is going to stay home? How are we going to make it financially?

All of those questions raise issues and opportunities for you to work towards something together, but also to have a plan, so life just doesn't happen to you. You may get surprised like the young man who came out of the ultrasound and said, "There's two. What are we going to do?" Well, you'll have twice as many children to love. It's still a wonderful thing.

Parents raising children must agree on a set of standards and consequences and present a united front to the children. Each time one parent is tired or gives in and allows the child to breach the family standards without consequences, it's like watching a blade of grass grow up through a tiny crack in a sidewalk. If you don't pull the weed out by its roots, over time the grass will crack the concrete sidewalk. Children will do that if you let them. If you're not unified as a couple, children will break you apart.

Children do it to get what they want and aren't emotionally mature enough to realize the damage they're doing. It's your job as a parent to make sure that doesn't happen. When our kids were growing up, the rule in our house was you can ask either parent about whatever you want to do, but once you got an answer, you were done asking. If you were told no, you didn't get to go to the other parent and ask the question to try to get a yes.

So how do you deal with that situation? As a parent, when your child asks you if they can do something, your response should always be, "have you asked" the other parent. If they say yes, then, respond, "whatever they said is the answer."

Then, children get to decide which parent to ask. Our children faced a challenge, because Linda was much more inclined to say no, but could sometimes be argued into yes. I was much more inclined to say yes but if I said no, there was no changing the answer. They could ask me why, and I would give them one answer. Every time they asked again after they got an answer cost them a weekend. They were more likely to get yes from me, but if they got no, the answer wasn't going to change.

My life experience suggests every generation faces different challenges. In high school in the 1970s, alcohol was the drug of choice. I knew of a few people who smoked marijuana, but if anyone at my high school used any other drug, it was something I never saw or heard anything about. There was no internet, and pornography wasn't readily available. From time to time, someone would come up with a *Playboy* magazine. By comparison to what's available today, no big deal. The sexual revolution began in the 1960s, but in 1970s small town America, premarital sex wasn't considered acceptable behavior, especially for young women.

By the early 1990s, when our children began attending high school, there were news reports of students dealing drugs in elementary schools in our area. Public displays of affection were common in high schools. The first AOL emails addresses appeared in 1993, and internet access required a hard-wired connection or an AOL dial-up connection. Both connections were too slow to allow for video and content-heavy websites you can access from a smartphone today.

The first cell phone with a camera came out in 2002. Apple released the first iPhone in 2007. 4G technology allowing rapid streaming of data and video from cell phones came out in 2010. By then, pornography was readily available to anyone with internet access.

If you're reading this book, the challenges you faced growing up were very different than those of your parents. Your children's challenges will be very different from yours. Moore's Law suggests the pace of technological change will continue to accelerate. If it does, or even if technology just changes on a straight-line basis, what challenges will your children face?

In the space below, on the left side, list your major challenges growing up and the technological changes you've experienced. On the right side, list what you think will be your children's major challenges and the technological changes they'll experience.

The Internet and social media allow your children access to pornography and allow people who would harm them access to your children. As a parent, you must keep up with the ever-changing technology kids use, and how your kids use it. One practical suggestion is to have an electronics basket in your bedroom. Every night, either before dinner or shortly after dinner, all electronic devices go in the basket and get locked in mom and dad's bedroom at night.

My parents told me nothing good happens after 10:00 pm. It's still true. Nothing good happens on electronic devices after 10:00 p.m. How many teenagers talk or text with their friends till 3:00 a.m. and then struggle to stay awake at school? How many of you did? What if you collected all of the devices after school until homework was done? Would your child's homework get done faster if there was no cell phone, XBox, TV, or music until it was done?

How many times have you seen parents and children sitting at the dinner table, all looking at an electronic device? When everyone's on a device, there is no communication and no connection. Family doesn't exist. You can create a new standard in your home, but if mom is on Facebook, Pinterest, or Instagram and Dad is watching ESPN (yes, those are stereotypes), how can they tell their kids to put down their devices?

If the two of you decide it's important to have dinner together and family time, consider device-free meals and device-free family time after dinner. Then, at the time you set, put all the devices in the electronics box for the night. If you set that standard as a family and enforce it consistently and evenly, you'll get the results you want.

Are your teenagers going to challenge you on it? Did *you* challenge *your* parents? Challenging parental authority is part of the process of growing up and developing independence. How you respond depends on the pattern of communication you've developed with your children. The pattern of communication you set with your children when they're young will be critically important when they're teenagers. If you don't talk to them regularly when they're young, they won't talk to you when they're teenagers.

Consider setting aside a time each week to talk to each child one on one, ask them questions, and listen. Talking with your children means 10 percent talking and 90 percent listening (without judgment, criticism, or punishment). Your children will learn to trust you to listen to them. Until they're heard, they won't hear you. Give them the opportunity to do that regularly. If you've built a high level of trust with your teenager over time, you should still be able to talk to them.

Part of the conversation may be about the difference between rights and privileges. In dealing with money, you had to learn the difference between needs and wants. Shoes are a need. Air Jordans are a want. Similar distinctions exist between rights and privileges.

In modern media, you hear a great deal about rights and very little about responsibilities. Every right has a corresponding responsibility. For example, the right to vote carries a responsibility to cast an informed ballot. The right to be safe in your home carries a responsibility not to break into someone else's home. Make sure you teach your children cause and effect, rights and responsibilities.

No child has a right to a cell phone, smartphone, laptop, or tablet. Getting and keeping any of those devices is a privilege they earn or lose based on conditions set by their parents. Driving before they reach legal adult age in their state is a privilege, not a right.

Turning 15 does not give a child a right to a learner's permit. Turning 16 does not give a child a right to a driver's license. Getting a driver's license does not give a child the right to a car of their own or to drive the family car. Those privileges should be earned and kept by adherence to conditions set by the parents.

If you set and enforce standards and consequences when they're young, your children learn to make better decisions; a skill that may save their lives when they're teenagers. In my ecclesiastical positions, I often met with families in their homes. Within five minutes of entering the home, I knew whether the parents or children were in charge. Any time the children ran the home, everyone was miserable, including the children.

Today, it's common to see young children screaming at and even hitting their parents. We had a different standard in our home. Our three children (bookend boys and a girl in the middle) could wrestle with, jump on, and tickle me at will. They knew never to touch their mother that way. She was off limits for anything other than hugs and kisses. If mom wanted to tickle them, they let her. Our children grew up respecting their mother and still do.

What effect do you think that had on how our sons treat their wives? How do you think that affected the way our daughter expected to be treated by her husband?

We always told our children if they were ever in an uncomfortable place or situation, or the driver had been drinking or was impaired, pick up the phone and call us. We will come get you. No punishment, no lecture, no anything. We just want you to be safe. Our children always knew they didn't have to worry about getting in trouble if they called us to come get them out of an uncomfortable situation.

Would you rather have your kids get in the car with a driver who's impaired or call you and say, "Mom, Dad, look, I didn't tell you I was coming to this party. I'm here. I shouldn't be. And the friend I came with has been drinking. I don't want to ride home with them. Will you come get me?" You have to lay a foundation of trust, respect, and communication to get that call.

If it sounds like a lot of work, you're right. Would you rather get that call or a knock on your door by the sheriff's deputy? "I'm sorry to inform you there's been an accident. Your son/daughter didn't make it." I never wanted that experience and hope none of you ever have it. At least if it ever happens, you may get some peace knowing you did everything you could to keep them safe.

As parents, you're not responsible for your children's choices. You are responsible to teach them correct principles and to be accountable for their decisions. If you teach young children the connection between choice and accountability with small decisions (like which of two outfits to wear to school), they will learn big decisions carry big consequences. When you've done the teaching, you've done all you can do.

The rest is really up to them, just like it was up to you when you were a teenager. Did you ever make a decision as a teenager you knew your parents wouldn't approve, and as an adult look back and wish you hadn't made? You may want to share some of those experiences with your children when they're old enough to face similar choices. I'm not suggesting you tell your children every stupid or embarrassing thing you did as a teenager.

I'm not even suggesting you tell them the story is about you. You can say, "I knew someone who . . ." and teach the principle. If your child asks, "is this about you" or "did you do that," just say, "It doesn't matter." The principle is the same. Your answer is true, and your child can decide for themselves if it was about you. If the story is about you, please don't say, "I had a friend who . . ." Your answer is a lie, and if your children even think you lied to them about a small thing, you cracked the foundation of their ability to trust you.

The first baby changes everything permanently, because no matter how old your children are, they're still your children. My wife never went to sleep until the last child was home, and she continues to worry about them today at ages 41, 37, and 33. She will worry about them until the day she dies. She's a mother, she loves them, and she will always worry.

I've seen moms and dads—especially after a divorce—who become their children's friends. Sorry, wrong answer. Until your children are 25, they need you to be a parent, not a friend. They need you to set standards and limits and teach them their decisions have consequences. That means telling them no and making it stick.

If you never hear your teenager say, "I hate you," you're not doing your job as a parent. When they turn 25, they can be your friend. Until then, be their parent.

Chapter 6

THINGS THAT CAN BREAK YOU

The primary causes of divorce are as varied as the sources you review. They include: infidelity, sex, money, communication, family/in-laws, religion, and friends. *www.marriage.com/advice/divorce/7-reasons-why-people-get-divorced/*

Another source lists the top five causes of divorce as lack of support in good times, money, communication, addiction, and adultery. *www.divorcemag.com/articles/surprisingly-common-causes-of-divorce/*

One other source cites infidelity, substance abuse, lack of commitment, conflict and arguing, growing apart, money, and marrying too young as causes of divorce. *www.businessinsider.com/why-people-get-divorced-2017-12#getting-married-too-young-7*

No matter what source you review, some life-altering events clearly can add enough stress to break an individual or a marriage, such as infidelity, death of a child or family member, mental and physical health challenges, job loss, abuse, and addiction. No one can predict which of these events they may have to endure as a marriage partner, when they will occur, or whether they will happen to you or your spouse.

Let's address some of the preventable ones and discuss how you can prepare for the ones you can't prevent in a way that draws you closer as a couple. Linda and I were high school sweethearts. We met a few days after she turned 16 and got engaged less than three months later. We got married when she was 17 and I was 18. At that time, Alabama law allowed a young woman to marry at 18 without a parent's consent. A young man had to be 19 to marry without a parent's consent. I suppose the Alabama legislature recognized women mature faster. (It was certainly true in our case).

We had our first child after my junior year of college, our second child while I was in law school and our third child while I was working ridiculous hours as a young lawyer. Linda and I both served in church positions that took a tremendous amount of time. When I started my law firm in 1992, our children were 15, 11, and 7. I worked the hours any new business owner does trying to build a business and provide for their family.

January 21, 2003 was one of the best—and worst – days of my life. I had graduated from Duke Law School twenty-one years before, was a business trial lawyer, and was in Michigan working on a case. Linda called and said, "We have our first grandson, and they named him after you, Brandon Stanley." I was overjoyed by his birth and humbled by his name, because our daughter had never said a word about naming her son after me. I was floating on air.

Every cell in my body was filled with light and energy for about 15 minutes until she called back and said, "There's something wrong with the baby. They've taken him to ICU." All the light and energy turned to fear and dread. My body felt like lead. The third call came a few hours later. "They think Brandon has a serious heart problem. They're transporting him to Rainbow Children's Hospital in Salt Lake City." I caught the next plane to Salt Lake City.

Brandon had open heart surgery when he was 4 days old, again when he was 4 months old, and died in my daughter's arms when he was eight months old. We flew our first grandson home to Florida, and I helped carry him to his grave. I will never forget the moment when I walked into the funeral home and saw his tiny metal casket. I loved playing baseball as a child and had gotten Brandon a baseball and placed it in his hands before they closed the casket.

I remember the red velvet comforter we laid the casket on to carry it to his grave. It was a beautiful fall day in Florida. I remember smelling the grass and feeling the wind on my face as we walked from the funeral home to the grave. I could hear people crying. I felt empty, because my little girl was hurting, and I couldn't do anything to fix it.

Fast forward seven years, and another grandson is born. Austin had none of Brandon's medical problems. He was a force of nature. Austin never bothered to learn to walk. He crawled, then he ran, then he climbed. He lived every moment full out. A hug from Austin made everything better, because he loved totally and unconditionally. He loved like there was no tomorrow, because for him there wasn't.

Our daughter was a night nurse who worked 7 p.m. to 7 a.m., so Linda went over and watched the children during the day so she could sleep. One day, she fixed lunch for the children and put out a bowl of grapes. Austin choked to death on a grape in front of my wife, my daughter, his two sisters, and his brother. Austin was four years old. For the second time in our lives, a light went out. For the second time in my life, I carried a grandson to his grave and buried him beside his big brother.

How do you handle the death of a child? What about two children? I can't imagine anything more difficult than losing a child. Even after losing two grandchildren, I don't pretend to understand what it was like for my daughter to lose two sons. Even as grandparents, their deaths were the hardest things we experienced as a couple. Brandon and Austin taught us life is fragile and fleeting, and far too precious to take for granted. We miss them every day, remember them in our prayers every night, and try to live every minute of our lives with joy to honor them.

The deck was stacked against our marriage. Teenage marriages fail at an even higher rate than the overall statistic of 40 to 50 percent of first marriages. How many couples do you know who married as young as we did and are still married? In spite of all we experienced, and how much each of us grew and changed, we grew even closer together.

We built strong enough bonds of love, trust, respect, and commitment to allow us to lean on each other in times of tragedy. We drew strength and comfort from each other and never looked for it anywhere else. At times, it might have been easier to walk away, but we began our marriage with a commitment to each other and to our future children.

Linda grew up a child of divorce. I grew up in a home where my parents stayed married but were miserable together. My wise young bride told me about a month before our wedding, "You don't have to do this, but if you do, it's forever." Neither of us wanted our children to have our childhood experiences. We were determined to show them a better way.

Let's talk about abuse. I have zero tolerance for abuse in any form; physical sexual, emotional, psychological, or other. Can an abusive marriage be changed and saved? It's possible, but not in the abusive home. Work on an abusive marriage should begin only after the abused person is out of the home, in a safe environment, and has an opportunity to heal. Once they begin to heal, they can decide if they want to try to create a healthy relationship with the abuser.

For a healthy relationship to be possible, the abuser must accept 100 percent responsibility for their actions and make whatever changes are necessary to prevent any further abuse. Required changes may include avoiding alcohol or other substances that reduce their self-control, avoiding people or circumstances that trigger the abuse, and getting whatever level of counseling is necessary.

Without those fundamental changes, I recommend against any effort to reconcile, because it will continue to be dangerous for the spouse or for any children subjected to abuse physically, sexually, or by witnessing abuse and seeing its effects.

Abuse should never happen. Americans need to adopt the airport philosophy of, "If you see something, say something." Don't pretend it didn't happen. Children can't protect themselves. They deserve to be protected. In many situations, women can't protect themselves. They deserve to be protected. Every person has the absolute right to be safe, loved, cherished, and protected.

Infidelity appears on virtually every list of the causes of divorce, because it's incredibly difficult to overcome. In Chapter 3, Plan Your Marriage, we talked about physical and emotional infidelity, and about your definition of infidelity. Emotional infidelity is forming an attachment with someone other than your spouse. It's inappropriate, whether it happens through social media, at work, at school, at the gym, or anywhere else. The lack of your needs being met at home is no excuse for infidelity.

If there are challenges in your marriage, talk about them honestly. Agree on solutions and live your commitments. Saying negative things about your spouse to someone else is a form of infidelity. Discussing your marriage problems with someone other than your spouse is disloyal, unless you're seeking assistance from a professional counselor or a member of the clergy. Talking negatively to your parents, siblings, friends, or co-workers about your marriage or your spouse is a breach of trust and cracks the foundation of your forever marriage.

The Law of Attraction applies to infidelity. If you don't understand the Law of Attraction, read or re-read *The Secret*, by Rhonda Byrne. In simplest terms, according to the Law of Attraction, the things you think about and talk about all of the time will be attracted into your life. If you spend a lot of time talking with your friends about their divorces, you'll attract divorce into your life.

If you spend time listening to people describe their marriage or their spouse in negative terms, you attract their negativity into your marriage.

If you describe your marriage or your spouse in a negative way, you attract more of the behavior. Most people will live up or down to your expectations. If you focus on things your partner does well, they'll do more of those things.

Here is a simple way to test the Law of Attraction:

Step 1   get a pack of yellow sticky notes.
Step 2   every day for a year, first thing in the morning or last thing at night, write down one positive quality or trait you love and appreciate about your spouse. (All 365 of them must be different!)
Step 3   leave each note somewhere your spouse is certain to see it.
Step 4   focus on that good quality or trait every time you think of your spouse that day.

Would your spouse feel different about you and your marriage at the end of a year where they got 365 love notes? Maybe they found the note on their mirror, in their underwear drawer, in a lunchbox, on their computer screen, or stuck on the steering wheel of their car. Every time they find a note, they'll know you thought something wonderful about them that day.

Do you think they might grow into the man or woman, husband or wife, you already see them as being? Reverse the questions. How would you feel if your spouse left a daily note of something they loved or appreciated about you? How excited would you be to find the note each day? How hard would you work to live up to their belief about you? If you both take the 365-day challenge, each of you will grow into your spouse's expectations, because it brings both of you joy.

The death of a family member or loss of a job affect the self-worth of a spouse who's lost a job or who has difficulty providing for their family. Those issues stress a marriage and add weight to the structure of the marriage. Trust, respect, and love are the three pillars of a forever marriage that bear all the burdens of life. They can bear a lot of weight. What they can't bear are fractures in the trust and respect pillars. When one of those pillars crumbles under the additional weight, the marriage fails.

Mental and physical health challenges create enormous physical, financial, and emotional burdens, whether they appear in the form of a child with special needs, an aging parent who needs care, a spouse or child who develops a disease or is seriously injured, or mental health issues. Those burdens fall on both spouses, but often one of them carries the bulk of the load. The woman often bears the tremendous physical and emotional burden of being a full-time caregiver.

My wife's mom, Jean, is a wonderful woman. When her aging parents were struggling, she moved back to their small town, moved in with them, and took care of them for several years while working a full-time job. I have enormous respect for her commitment and sacrifice, but also saw the toll it took on her. I'm grateful she endured and hope when my time comes (sometime in the next 60 or so years), our children will take as good care of me.

> ### *Contempt, criticism, and control (three C's) devastate marriages.*

Contempt is an attitude or belief your spouse is beneath you, inadequate, or not worthy of your love or respect. Contempt amplifies feelings of inadequacy our society already fosters. Many people feel inadequate because they don't match up to A-list Hollywood stars in terms of looks, height, weight, body image, job, money, and so on.

One of our fundamental fears as human beings is that we're not enough to be worthy of love. Those clouds of self-doubt hide the truth. Every one of us is amazing and beautiful and special in our own way. We're worthy to be loved exactly as we are. We don't have to change to be loved, and no one else can change us. The only person any of us can change is ourselves. Like Benjamin Franklin, we should be engaged in a constant process of growth and self-improvement throughout our lives.

If you develop a habit of 30 minutes of daily exercise now, how much difference will it make in your quality of life when you're 75? What if you maintain a reasonable weight and level of fitness and flexibility starting now? You can either develop those habits and continue to enjoy a strong, capable, flexible body, or not. You limit your future options by the choices you make today.

Marriage works the same way. Marriage is a living organism that either grows or dies a little each day. The little things you do and say, or don't do and don't say, either strengthen the foundation of your forever marriage, or crack it. How solid it becomes over time is entirely up to you. Contempt cracks the foundation and can shatter it completely. Why would anyone want to be with someone who held them in contempt?

Criticism is contempt's first cousin and comes in many forms. Some people try to make themselves feel better or improve themselves by criticizing or belittling others. Others try to make themselves feel better by comparing themselves to the object of their scorn. In reality, criticism of others reveals your own character. Would you rather be around someone who criticizes others or someone who lifts others?

If you want love, joy, passion, and connection in your marriage, avoid criticizing the people you love. They're extremely vulnerable to the things you say and the way you say them. Connection requires emotional vulnerability. Criticism closes your spouse off emotionally to avoid the pain your words inflict. When they close down, you lose connection.

The Law of Attraction works on negative thoughts and emotions, too. If you constantly criticize your spouse and think of all of their negative qualities, they'll probably live down to your expectation. I remember my dad listened to an old country song that included these lyrics, "I'd rather be sorry for something I did than for something that I didn't do."

If you constantly accuse your spouse of something they didn't do, they're already being punished. Why shouldn't they go ahead and do it? They're already taking the pain, they might as well get the pleasure. Don't project your insecurities onto your spouse.

Criticism also may include what men consider nagging; asking them to do something over and over. ("You asked me six months ago. I'll get around to it.") Another form of criticism is when your spouse does something you ask but doesn't do it the way you do or wanted it done and you complain or redo the job.

We struggled with that for years. Linda keeps an immaculate house (for which I'm very grateful) and knows exactly how she wants things done. She would ask for help and from time to time, I even helped without being asked. I'd do the job, and she would go behind me and redo it. When she did, in my mind, my time spent on the task was wasted. I'm logical, linear, and practical, so that drove me nuts.

Now that we're empty-nesters, most nights we do the dishes together. I wash, she rinses, and then she wipes down the counters. (I never learned to do it to her satisfaction). When the last dish is washed, I'm finished. Our new rule is Linda can ask me to do something and let me do it my way or do it herself. Problem solved!

Control is marriage poison. A man can be controlling physically or financially. A woman can be controlling financially or through access to sex or intimacy. All of those methods are equally wrong. Control is toxic to a marriage, because it communicates a lack of respect for your spouse.

To have a forever marriage, you need to walk side-by-side; neither in front of nor behind the other. You don't have to be equal in all things. At times, each of you will lead in different things, but at the end of the day, you walk side-by-side and hand-in-hand. Getting the most out of your marriage means each of you uses your skills, gifts, and talents to complement the other.

Can a marriage overcome infidelity?

A marriage can survive infidelity, but probably only once, and only if the cheater's spouse can forgive them completely. In every aspect of marriage, an ounce of prevention is worth a pound of cure. In infidelity, the price of discipline is measured in ounces, the price of regret in tons. Doing the exercises in this book and taking the time to do the little things daily can build a protective barrier around your marriage.

But no matter what you do, sometimes your spouse will be unfaithful. It's not your fault, and only you can decide whether you can or should forgive them. The second question is easier to answer than the first. Should you forgive them? Yes, for your own good. If you don't forgive, you'll become bitter and angry.

Carrie Fisher, who played Princess Leia in *Star Wars*, once said, "Bitterness is like drinking poison and waiting for the other person to die." Forgiving infidelity doesn't necessarily mean staying in the marriage. It means letting go of the pain, anger, and bitterness, so you can have joy in your life, whether with your current spouse or someone else.

As young newlyweds, my very wise bride told me if I ever stopped looking at attractive women, she'd know I was doing something with one of them. She also told me that if I ever felt the need to be with anyone else, go ahead, but please have the courtesy to divorce her first. To her, being unfaithful was the most hurtful thing one person could do to another. (I realize every day what an extraordinary woman she is).

If the spouse who's been cheated on decides to try to save the marriage, repairing the damage done will require a tremendous amount of commitment and patience by the unfaithful spouse. Their marriage was a jigsaw puzzle they assembled together, built with 1,000 tiny pieces in many different shades of green to form a beautiful pasture and forest scene.

Before the infidelity, the completed puzzle sat on the kitchen table, quiet, complete and serene, and represented the twin pillars of trust and respect supporting their love for each other. Infidelity tore all 1,000 pieces apart and scattered them around the house. The unfaithful spouse has to be patient enough to rebuild the trust and respect they shattered by spending as much time as it takes to find and put all 1,000 pieces back together.

During that process, the unfaithful spouse has no right to make demands or have any expectations of their partner other than fidelity. Putting together a few pieces doesn't give them the right to expect immediate trust or emotional intimacy. They have to commit to complete fidelity and do the work, no matter how long it takes. If they're not willing to commit to complete fidelity or if they're serial cheaters, pack up and leave. You can't have a forever marriage with them.

A relationship based on trust is fragile. As a trial lawyer, I once participated in a legal organization called the Inns of Court. A very distinguished federal district judge who led our group explained every lawyer comes to court with a trust bank (imagine a piggy bank).

Each time the lawyer tells the judge the facts and the evidence supports those facts, he or she gets a small deposit into the trust bank. Each time the lawyer tells the judge the law and the judge's research confirms that's the law, he or she gets another small deposit into the trust bank. Over time, the lawyer builds up a bank of trust with the judge, so when things aren't clear-cut, the lawyer with the biggest trust bank gets the benefit of the doubt.

Then came the warning and the lesson. The judge said the first time a lawyer tells the judge the facts or the law and it's not right, he or she just broke the trust bank. He or she has to start over by picking up the pieces of the trust bank and putting them back together before they can even begin to make new deposits.

That's exactly what infidelity does in marriage. It destroys the trust bank. If the marriage is going to survive, the unfaithful spouse must be willing to reassemble the trust bank one piece at a time and then, make a tremendous number of small daily deposits in the bank.

Complete fidelity is essential to a forever marriage. I don't believe it's possible for an open or polyamorous marriage to be lasting, successful, or even satisfying for the participants. Marriage involves two people and yet 40 to 50 percent fail. Adding participants complicates relationships by orders of magnitude, because of the level of perfection required to meet everyone's needs.

To make an open or polyamorous marriage long-lasting requires at least two perfect people with no insecurities, jealousy, or other human failings. Since only one perfect person ever lived on the earth, the odds of finding two perfect people and putting them in the same relationship are exactly zero. The odds of finding three or more are less than zero.

When you decide to be married, you also have to decide to be physically and emotionally faithful to your spouse. Absolute physical and emotional fidelity are essential to a forever marriage.

Chapter 7

MEN AND WOMEN ARE DIFFERENT

Ladies, have you ever noticed men can only think about one thing at a time? If they're watching sports, playing on the computer, or reading a book, you don't exist. You have to get their undivided attention for them to hear you at all. That's because men and women are different. They think and communicate differently.

Men tend to be fixers. They want to solve problems and move on; and because they can only think about one thing at a time, they don't multitask very well. They want to solve the problem in front of them, so they can get back to what they want to do.

Men, has your lady ever started to tell you about a challenge or problem she had that day? You told her how to solve the problem, and she wasn't happy with you? Ladies, when you told your man about your problem or challenge, did you want him to solve your problem (or did you already know the answer)?

He thought you wanted him to solve your problem, because that's what men do. He didn't understand you just wanted to be heard and have your feelings validated. You weren't broken and didn't need to be fixed. All you wanted him to do was listen.

Linda and I lived that story daily for the first 20 years of our marriage. I'm a trial lawyer; a left-brain, logical, linear thinker. I get paid to solve other people's problems quickly. My job is to get from point A to Point B as fast as possible, and I'm not terribly patient. I want it done, and I want it done now. (How else did I handle working two jobs while in college full-time and trying to spend time with my wife and new baby?) Linda knew how busy I was (four hours of sleep was a good night), so I assumed she wouldn't tell me about a problem unless she wanted me to solve it for her.

She would begin to tell me about something she did, some experience or challenge she'd had, or some problem she'd run into, and I'd tell her how to fix it. My solutions were simple, clear and correct, and she would get upset with me. I stayed confused until I read John Gray's book, *Men Are from Mars, Women Are from Venus*.

I literally rolled on the floor laughing, thinking he wrote the book about us! I learned a whole new skillset about how to communicate with the woman I loved. She just wanted me to be quiet, pay attention, and nod periodically to let her know I was awake. She was happier than she'd been in all the years of me offering her solutions. Listening also eliminated any possibility of something stupid coming out of my mouth and making her even more upset.

An experience very early in our marriage should have clued me in to Dr. Gray's wonderful idea. Unfortunately, it didn't. I was a little slow on the uptake. We went to bed one night as newlyweds - somewhere in our first year of marriage. Everything was fine between us when I went to sleep, but when we woke up the next morning, she wasn't speaking to me. I wondered, *Did I say an old girlfriend's name in my sleep? Did I roll over and hit her? I mean, what in the world did I do wrong? I was asleep!*

After asking, "What's wrong honey," about 20 times, she finally told me. "I spent 30 minutes pouring out my heart to you last night and then realized you'd been asleep the whole time!" To my credit, I resisted the urge to say, "At any point during that 30 minutes, did you think to ask for my opinion or let me say anything?" I didn't do that—probably the only reason I lived.

We came up with a new communication rule - it doesn't count if I'm horizontal. When I'm horizontal, if something very interesting isn't going on I'm Nicolas Cage's car Eleanor from the movie *Gone in 60 Seconds*. I'm asleep before she finds a comfortable position. She learned if she wants to have a conversation with me, I have to be sitting or standing. If I'm horizontal, whatever she says doesn't count.

In my work with couples and adults over many years, some common themes emerged. Many men describe an ability to fall asleep almost instantly. Women multitask very well. A woman can be making dinner with a baby on her hip, the phone on one ear, and tell children two rooms away to stop fighting. Her brain is a multi-channel device. Perhaps that's why when women describe the inability to go to sleep, they frequently use the same language, "My mind is just swirling." They can't stop thinking about all the things they need to do or are concerned about.

Because men can only think about one thing at a time, they also can think about nothing at all. A comedian named Mark Gungor has a hilarious explanation of some of the differences between how men and women think and communicate. Five minute and twelve-minute versions can be found at *https://www.youtube.com/watch?v=SkDYDSz616I* (for the five-minute version) and

https://www.youtube.com/watch?v=kFd2bXch6b4 (for the twelve-minute version). The longer version is even more fun and informative.

Linda and I are perfect illustrations of those differences. I've lived and slept well for over 60 years with a simple philosophy. When I get in bed at night, I've fixed all the things I can that day and refuse to worry about the rest. I'll deal with them tomorrow. I worry about nothing I can't fix. Linda worries about everything, whether she can fix it or not. It balances out, and we each have a roughly equal amount of worry. She just carries mine for me.

When your lady tells you about a challenge or problem, she doesn't want you to solve the problem or fix her, because she's not broken. She already knows the solution. She just wants to be heard and have her feelings validated. All you need to say is something simple like, "That must have been really difficult. Is there anything you'd like me to do?"

She'll say no almost all of the time and think you're wonderful and understanding. She got what she needed emotionally from the conversation. She needed to talk and to share. She just needed you to listen. Men, all you have to do to win is be quiet. What a wonderful rule!

Ladies, communicating with men means understanding we don't get clues. Men don't get small, medium, large, or huge clues, and we're not supposed to. When you need to communicate in clues, talk to your girlfriends. They'll understand completely. No man ever spent hours analyzing every word, tone, and gesture in a conversation, along with what wasn't said and what every one of those things meant, or what the other person might have meant. Not once, not ever. And he has no clue why you do it.

If you ask a man what he wants, you may not like the answer (especially if you're home alone with him), but he'll tell you. If you ask him what he wants for dinner, he'll say whatever you fix or wherever you want to go. He just wants to eat, so both answers are true. He really doesn't care.

It's very different when a man asks a woman what she wants to do for date night or where she wants to eat. If she says, "whatever you plan is fine," is that an honest answer? No! She knows exactly what she wants to do or where she wants to eat.

She thinks she's given him plenty of clues, and he should know. That creates several problems. First, men don't get clues. Second, men can't read minds (and you'd be horrified if they could). Third, her answer wasn't honest.

The third is the most important. She knows it's not true. He knows it's not true, and he knows she knows it's not true. Reduced to basics, she just lied to him, and they both know it. She just cracked the foundation of his trust for her; one of the pillars supporting their marriage. To have a forever marriage, you work every day to strengthen those pillars, not crack them.

In addition to being destructive, the lie set you both up to be unhappy. The woman didn't get what she wanted, and the man got an unhappy woman. Ladies, with few exceptions, your man doesn't care if you look like a movie star. He just wants you to be happy. If you had been honest and told him what you wanted, 99 times out of a 100, he would have agreed.

Ladies, the secret to getting what you want from your man is to get his undivided attention. Whether he's watching TV, playing a video game, on the computer, or reading a book, get into his personal space. Get face-to-face. Put your hands on both sides of his face, look right in his eyes, and tell him exactly what you want. "I want you to take me to see this movie and to Baskin Robbins." It's that easy to get what you want.

Why? We draw much of our satisfaction from you being happy, fulfilled, grateful, and joyful. And yes, because when you're not happy, our lives are miserable! Why do something that makes both of you miserable? Tell him what you want, so he can win. By the way, if you don't use this method from now on, and don't get what you want from your man, it's your fault!

Hopefully, you have a man who's strong enough if you ask for something he really doesn't want to do, he'll say no, and you respect him enough not to pout. You're not going to get your way all the time (and you shouldn't want to), but it means you're going to get what you really want; a forever marriage full of love, joy, passion, and connection.

Each person has a unique communication style reflected in everything they do. Many businesses use personality tests in hiring and job placement to identify the communication style of each applicant. The human resources departments use the test results to hire the right people and get the right people into each position. Good managers use the test results to help them understand the work preferences and communication styles of each of their employees. Used correctly, the tests help put employees in fulfilling positions where they'll be most productive.

You can use those tests to strengthen your forever marriage. You and your spouse should go online, research which test you want to take (many of them are free), and each of you take and score your test separately. If you're not married yet, taking one of those tests before saying I do or while planning the marriage would be ideal. If you're already married, take one anyway. Anything you can do to strengthen your communication with your spouse strengthens your marriage.

Understanding each other's communication style will be even more important when you have children. The two of you need to communicate effectively, and each of your children will have a communication style different from each of you and different from each other child. Many of the tests can be taken by children to give you information on each child's communication style and needs.

The business-based general personality tests are an excellent starting point, but your education doesn't end there. Communication takes on special meaning and even greater importance in the intimate relationships that produce all the real love, joy, and happiness in life, between spouses and between parents and children. Those relationships add extra complexity to communication.

A wonderful book called *The Five Love Languages* teaches intimate communication and offers a free online self-assessment. It teaches that we tend to show love in the way we receive love. The five love languages are: physical touch, words of affirmation, quality time, acts of service, and receiving gifts. For example, if your love language is receiving gifts, you will tend to show love by giving gifts.

If your spouse or child's love language is quality time, they don't feel loved by receiving gifts, and you feel frustrated by their lack of response. They show love to you by spending quality time with you, which doesn't feel like love to you.

Linda and I struggled until we learned these principles. My love languages are physical touch first and words of affirmation second. Her primary love language is acts of service. I hugged her to show I loved her, because that's how I feel loved. She didn't feel loved, because it wasn't an act of service.

She did the laundry, made dinner, or cleaned up the house to show she loved me. I didn't feel loved, because touch or words of affirmation are my love languages. We loved each other for years before we learned how to communicate our love effectively. We couldn't learn, because we never knew people could have different love languages.

Do you think it might reduce the divorce rate if couples learned each other's communication styles and love languages? You're like two people sitting together at a table one speaking French and one speaking Russian. No matter how loving the words, they have no idea what the other person is thinking or feeling.

Ladies, men usually aren't as sensitive or emotionally intelligent as you, but they feel it when you pull away emotionally. When they feel it, they ask you "What's wrong honey?" What do you say most of the time, "nothing." Is that true? Your husband knows it's not true. You know it's not true. He knows you know it's not true. Every dishonest answer cracks the pillar of trust in your marriage.

If he asks what's wrong enough times to get beyond "nothing," what's typically the second answer? "I don't know." At least it's honest. A very logical follow-up question from him would be, "If you don't know what's wrong, why should I?" If he's smart, he's going to chew that question carefully, swallow it, and make sure not to let any part slip out of his mouth or show on his face!

A better answer to, "What's wrong honey" might be, "I'm not ready to talk about it yet." That's brilliantly, brutally, absolutely honest. He knows he's in trouble, but at least you told the truth. You didn't crack the pillar of trust in your marriage. Men, if your lady gives you that answer, be wise enough to respect it and say, "Okay, when you're ready to talk, I'm ready to listen."

That answer changes everything. When you're ready, you can have the conversation, and you avoided using emotional distance as a way to control or punish your spouse. You don't want to be controlled or manipulated. Neither does your man.

Chapter 8

A Diamond Marriage: BECAUSE MARRIAGE SHOULD BE FOREVER TOO

Every couple who says "I do" believes they will be together forever, and their marriage will be happy and fulfilling. They expect every day to be filled with love, joy, passion, and connection. Then life happens, and their marriage doesn't live up to their expectations. They question whether they should have gotten married at all, or whether they married the right person. They didn't ask the right questions before they got married.

They didn't ask the questions "Before You Say I Do." They didn't avoid the problems caused by the wedding culture in America. They didn't spend enough time, money, and energy planning their marriage. They didn't think through what happens after the honeymoon, or what happens with our baby, or my children, your children, and our children. They didn't think about the things that can break a marriage.

One or both of them neglected the critical component of absolute fidelity in marriage. They didn't discuss and plan for the problems that are a natural part of life and all of us will experience at some point; death, job loss, or health issues. They were never taught men and women are different; they think, communicate and react differently. They're supposed to be different. Without those differences, there's no passion, joy, or connection. The differences are the basis for love, not a reason for divorce.

So instead of having a diamond marriage that lasts forever, they fall by the wayside. They become another victim of our disposable society, a number in the divorce statistics. Divorce financially and emotionally destroys the couple and devastates their children. Children of divorce are two times more likely to attempt suicide, three hundred percent more likely to need psychiatric counseling in any given year, exhibit more high-risk and addictive behaviors, have more educational problems and tend to have lower lifetime earnings.

Divorce is so prevalent in American society if it were a disease, it wouldn't just be an epidemic, it would be a pandemic, and it's tearing the country apart. We have families with no father or no mother. We have step-parent problems with my kids, your kids, and our kids that create unique problems.

In blended families, the children often were raised with different standards and family traditions. How do you allow the children to hold onto family traditions that are part of their security and blend those traditions to create a new family? That's part of the sex, money, children, and religion conversation before you say "I do" to a second or subsequent marriage.

On a side note, if you've been divorced more than once, you need to step back and stop dating until you figure out why your relationships failed. In almost all situations, start by acknowledging at least some personal responsibility for the failure of the relationships.

In cases of abuse, that's not true, but the advice is still sound. If you've been married to abusers more than once, you need to figure out why you keep attracting or being attracted to abusers. You have patterns you need to identify and break before you or your children get permanently broken.

Children in blended families often feel the step-parent favors his or her own children and applies different standards to them. Even if there really is a single standard equally enforced by both parents, it's rarely the children's perception. And for all of us—especially children—perception is reality. The single set of standards should be part of the sex, money, children and religion discussion before you say "I do" to that second or subsequent marriage.

Children of divorce often are subject to different standards in the homes of their now-divorced parents. The parent with more money may consciously or unconsciously try to buy the children's affection with material things or activities the other parent can't afford.

Children are human, too (even teenagers), and instinctively seek freedom. Since children view rules or consequences as restrictions, they often favor the home with the fewest rules. The parent who lets them do whatever they want whenever they want (or even parties with them) becomes the favorite. By the way, a parent who parties with their children who are under 25 isn't a parent at all; they're an overgrown child.

One or both parents may deliberately try to alienate the children from the other parent. I know of one couple who fought constantly while they were married. Once they divorced, they got along better than they ever had while they were married - until one of them found someone new. Almost immediately, the now-rejected ex-spouse began to vilify the other spouse and their new partner. Despite being told by professional counselors the comments were damaging the children, they didn't stop.

Unfortunately, divorce courts are very limited in their ability to protect children from any of the problems listed above, except in extreme cases, and even then, often only after the children have suffered substantial physical or emotional injury. Anything we can do to change the divorce statistics and provide a safe, loving home for every child is worthwhile.

Imagine if every child in America grew up in a loving home with their mother and their father. How different would our nation be? How different would our world be?

Marriage is essential to the well-being of our children and to our emotional fulfillment as human beings. Stable families build stable communities, stable states, and stable nations. How would the divorce statistics change in the next generation if more of our children grew up with a model of a loving, happy, lasting marriage?

When our youngest son was born in 1985, we brought him home from the hospital to the same house we lived in the day he graduated from high school. His friends were amazed he had lived in the same house his whole life and asked him, "You mean you've lived there with your mom and dad-- your real mom and dad-- the whole time?"

Our daughter was born in 1981, and many of her high school friends came from broken homes. They didn't have a strong male figure in their life, so I became Dad to many of her friends. To this day, 20 years later, when several of them see me they run up and hug me and say, "I need a dad hug." Kids need stability, and we owe it to our children to give it to them.

Every marriage *can* be saved. Not every marriage *should* be saved. The vast majority of marriages can be and should be saved, and we owe it to our children to save them. In most cases, the incidents leading to divorce boil down to lack of education on the things we've talked about in this book, or selfishness. Once you decide to have children, it's not about you—it's about your children. It's a hard road, but you chose the road.

When you work through challenges in a marriage, when you love, communicate, commit and do the things necessary to make a marriage survive and thrive, you teach your children that hard work and commitment matter, integrity is critical, families are forever, and there really can be love at home.

We hope for love between a man and woman, love between a husband and wife, love between partners, love for their children. You're not going to live in a world of sunshine and roses where there's never a problem. You probably shouldn't want to, because we learn and grow when we struggle: not when life is easy. Think back - have you learned more from your successes or your failures?

When we're pushed and stretched and think we can't do one more thing or go on one more minute and we do, we grow stronger. To develop stronger muscles or run longer or faster, we practice, push ourselves, stretch our limits, and, sometimes, we suffer. We don't get stronger by lifting the same amount of weight for the same number of reps and sets each time.

We get stronger by pushing ourselves (or, sometimes, being pushed by life). Our mental and emotional muscles grow the same way, when we push past our limits. We need to consciously develop a plan to grow individually, as part of a couple, and as a parent; a personal self-development plan.

A forever marriage is intentional. It's deliberate, planned, and worked on daily. Graphite and diamond each are composed of carbon atoms, but they're arranged differently. The arrangement of carbon atoms in graphite makes it so slippery it's used as a lubricant. When you place carbon atoms under enough heat and enough pressure for enough time, they rearrange into a diamond—the hardest known natural substance.

Diamonds have become a symbol of marriage. In the late 1940s, one of the diamond sellers came up with an advertising slogan "A Diamond is Forever" that linked diamonds and romantic love. In 1971, Sean Connery played James Bond in the movie *Diamonds Are Forever*. If marriages lasted forever, diamonds would be a perfect symbol.

I founded the Relationship Magic Academy to teach couples how to transform the marriage they have into the marriage they want. To make that transformation possible, I created The Diamond Relationship Formula™.

The Diamond Relationship Formula™ is a series of simple, practical steps anyone can do to transform their relationship, and contains a mathematical formula that allows them to measure the condition of their relationship now and measure its improvement over time as they work through the course.

The formula is QR=QQCC™. You can learn more about the formula at *www.relationshipmagicacademy.com*.

I simply couldn't stand to see what divorce was doing to children anymore. My mission is to save a million marriages in the next five years. I hope this book has helped you and provided you with tools you can put to work in your marriage today, to make it lasting, loving, and joyful. I wish you and your spouse love, joy, passion, and connection every day for the rest of your lives.

Marriage Planning Form

Write the answers to these questions in your personal journal, whether it's on paper or electronic. The more detailed you are the more successful you'll be and the more love, joy, passion and connection you'll enjoy every day.

If you think this sounds like a lot of work, it is! You're following the 90/10 formula. You're going to work much harder planning your marriage than you did planning your wedding. Your wedding lasted a few hours and your marriage needs to last a lifetime. Doesn't it make sense to put more effort into the marriage than the wedding?

Describe Your Ideal Day as a Married Couple.

Describe your marriage in 1 year, 5, 10, 20 and 30 years. Include goals for each of you and as a couple in the following areas: Physical, Emotional, Educational, Geographical (where will you live), Financial and Marriage.

What will you do to make those goals happen?

What are your interim goals that are steps to the bigger goals?

What actions will you need to take over time to achieve those goals?

How will you celebrate when you achieve each goal?

How will you reward yourselves and each other?

How much time will each of you commit each day to your marriage plan and goals and to each other?

How often will you meet and counsel together to check your progress and stay on track?

What action will you take RIGHT NOW to create excitement and momentum?

PUT DOWN YOUR PAPER AND DO IT NOW!

RELATIONSHIP MAGIC ACADEMY™
Transform the Relationship You Have Into the Relationship You Want

35 Must-Read Books for You and Your Teens

If your children read these books, they will receive a more useful education than they can get from any college degree. You should read them, too. Note which books you already, have, which you plan to purchase, and when you plan to read them yourself and/or have your teenager read them.

	OWN	BUY	When to Read	When to Give to Our Teenager
Think & Grow Rich				
How to Win Friends & Influence People				
Dave Ramsey's Complete Guide to Monday				
The Aladdin Factor				
The Magic of Thinking Big				
The Magic of Getting What you Want				
The Magic of Thinking Success				
Rich Dad, Poor Dad				
The Science of Influence				
Talking the Winners Way				
The 12 Month Millionaire				
The Greatest Salesman in the World				
Any book by Og Mandino				
7 Habits of Highly Successful People				
The 8th Habit				
The Purpose Driven Life				
Treasury of Quotes				
Cashflow Quadrant				
The Ultimate Gift				
No B.S. Time Management for Entrepreneurs				
Motivation Manifesto				
EntreLeadership				
Awaken the Giant Within				
Money: Master the Game				
Any book by Anthony Robbins				
Eat That Frog				
Any book by Brian Tracy				
The Secret by Rhonda Byrne				
How to Master the Art of Selling				
Scientific Advertising				
Crushing It				
The 5 Love Languages				
The Big Leap				
The Master Key System				
The Inner Game of Success				
Biographies of Successful People				

Copyright © 2018 Relationship Magic Academy, LLC. All Rights Reserved

www.ingramcontent.com/pod-product-compliance
Lightning Source LLC
LaVergne TN
LVHW011954070526
838202LV00054B/4915